GETTING STA
WITH TECH E̶T̶H̶I̶C̶S

An introduction to ethics
and ethical behaviours
for IT professionals

by Gillian Arnold, Darren Dalcher,
Catherine Flick, Neil Gordon, Bernd
Carsten Stahl and Robert Tripp

TABLE OF CONTENTS

ABOUT THE AUTHORS

Gillian Arnold is a prominent figure in the British IT sector, known for her leadership and advocacy for women in technology. She has held significant roles, including President of BCS, The Chartered Institute for IT, and was the Chair of the BCS Women Specialist Group. She has been recognised multiple times as one of the most influential women in UK IT by *Computer Weekly*. She also founded Tectre, a company focused on diversity in tech, after a 22-year career at IBM.

Darren Dalcher is a Professor in Strategic Project Management at Lancaster University Management School and the Director of the National Centre for Project Management. He has published over 300 refereed papers and more than 30 books, and serves as the Editor-in-Chief of Wiley's *Journal of Software: Evolution and Process*. Recognised as one of the top 10 influential experts in project management by the Association for Project Management, Dalcher has a significant impact on both academia and industry.

Catherine Flick is a Professor of Ethics and Games Technology of the Staffordshire Games Institute at the University of Staffordshire who has a background in History and Philosophy of Science and Computer Science and a PhD in Computer Ethics. Having played video games since she was very small, she has since carved out a specific niche area of research looking at the ethical and social impact of games. She also has significant expertise in the ethics of emerging technologies, including cryptocurrencies and blockchain, artificial intelligence and machine learning, and social media, along with interests in online safety and online child protection, and responsible research and innovation.

Neil Gordon is a Professor in Computer Science at the University of Hull, a National Teaching Fellow, and a Principal Fellow of AdvanceHE. He has produced several reports for AdvanceHE, in particular on how technology-enhanced learning can enable flexible pedagogy, on the role of assessment in education, and on ways to address issues in retention and attainment in computing education. His research interests include applications of computer science to enable true technology-enhanced learning, issues around sustainable development, as well as more discipline-specific work on applications of computer algebra and formal methods. Neil chairs the BCS ICT Ethics specialist group and the International Federation of Information Processing Working group 9.2 on Social Accountability and Computing.

Bernd Carsten Stahl is a Professor of Critical Research in Technology at the School of Computer Science at the University of Nottingham where he leads the Responsible Digital Futures group (responsible-digital-futures.org/). His interests cover philosophical issues arising from the intersections of business, technology and information. This includes ethical questions of current and emerging ICTs, critical approaches to information systems and issues related to responsible research and innovation.

Robert Tripp is a management consultant specialising in technology-led change, particularly in the banking sector. As founder and Managing Director of Tripple Consulting, he combines deep technical expertise with a rare ability to translate complex systems into clear, actionable insights for business leaders. His current work focuses on making banking better either by helping finance sector not-for-profits grow and develop or by helping for-profits implement their projects more ethically.

PREFACE

This book brings together the insights of leading figures from across the technology landscape – academics, consultants and industry veterans – each of whom has made a distinctive contribution to the ethical development of digital systems. From Gillian Arnold's pioneering leadership in inclusion and diversity in tech, to Darren Dalcher's internationally respected expertise in strategic project management, the authors offer grounded perspectives shaped by decades of professional impact. Catherine Flick contributes deep knowledge at the intersection of games, emerging technologies and online safety; Neil Gordon bridges computing education, ethics and sustainable development; Bernd Carsten Stahl draws on a rich philosophical tradition to interrogate responsible innovation; and Robert Tripp offers field-tested insight from the heart of financial systems and AI ethics. Together, they make the case for a more thoughtful, accountable and socially responsive future for technology practitioners.

What makes this book distinct is the way it develops a comprehensive yet grounded approach to tech ethics, guiding readers through a complete ethical journey that mirrors the real-world lifecycle of technology. Beginning with an accessible introduction and a solid grounding in the foundations of tech ethics, it moves from the individual – through professional ethics – into the team and institutional setting in organisational ethics and diversity. It then broadens its lens to explore societal responsibilities, before turning toward proactive, forward-facing strategies in sustainable and ethical practices and navigating emerging technologies. The final chapter, Future Directions in Tech Ethics, consolidates the lessons and tools offered throughout, inviting readers to continue shaping ethical practice in a dynamic landscape. This structure, combined with a strong emphasis on practical implementation inside IT departments, makes the book uniquely valuable: a resource not just for reflection but for action.

Whether you're a student beginning your journey in computing, an early-career developer navigating real-world complexities for the first time, or a seasoned professional seeking to refresh your ethical lens, this book is written with you in mind. It recognises the full spectrum of roles that make up our industry – from software engineers to UX designers, IT managers to data analysts, infrastructure leads to policy architects. In a field as broad and fast-moving as ours, ethics must be practical, inclusive and adaptable. Our hope is that this book offers not only insights, but usable tools – supporting reflective, responsible practice for anyone shaping the digital world.

1 INTRODUCTION

Neil Gordon

This introductory chapter is structured in three interwoven strands. First, we consider a well-known ethical case – the UK Post Office's Horizon scandal – to illustrate how ethical blind spots in technology can have devastating real-world consequences, setting the tone for why tech ethics is not optional. Second, we consider how, in today's data-driven world, emerging technologies like generative artificial intelligence (AI) are increasingly embedded in high-stakes domains such as healthcare, education and policing, often without ethical scrutiny. Third, we outline the book's practical mission: to equip professionals across the tech ecosystem with tools, questions and frameworks for ethical decision-making – not through abstract theory, but through grounded, actionable strategies. We preview the journey ahead, from individual responsibility to global impact, and invite readers to see ethics not as a bolt-on, but as central to building technology that truly serves society.

In 1999, a software system called Horizon was introduced by the UK Post Office to manage financial transactions across its network of post offices. It was a modern improvement on the previous system (Capture), being automated and efficient. However, as the system was used, and based on the accounting data coming out of the system, apparently hundreds of sub-postmasters were guilty of financial misconduct – errors no human could explain, but the computer insisted were real. Careers were shattered, reputations destroyed, lives devastated. Years later it emerged: the system was wrong. It had been wrong all along. This example is explored more in Chapter 4.

Horizon isn't just a story about software bugs. It's a case study in what happens when technology, organisations and ethical blind spots collide. You don't need to be a philosopher. But you do need to know how to spot a potential ethical iceberg before your ship hits it. That's what this book is here for: to help you get started – not just in tech, but in thinking ethically about tech.

Today's IT professionals work in a complex world, with complex interacting systems. Data is driving this 4th industrial revolution. Generative AI and other emerging technologies are used to make hiring decisions, calculate credit scores and educate from school and college to university and into CPD. These complex data-driven systems are increasingly used for critical applications, such as health, controlling autonomous vehicles and in policing and military applications. New technologies arrive with fanfare but increasingly with little critique or scrutiny. Insufficient numbers of people pause to ask fundamental questions about where we should build this, who could be harmed and what happens if it all goes wrong.

Given the role of software at the heart of so much of today's world, the consequences of failures in software can be disastrous for individuals, companies and beyond. Software has been identified as responsible for accidents and for intentional harm, too. Examples of accidents include the Boeing plane crashes, where faulty sensors and the consequential decision of the plane control systems led to crashes. Intentional harm includes examples such as the diesel scandal, of car companies using software control systems to alter engine performance, to evade and corrupt emissions tests and thus lead to more pollution in the environment. Of course, harm goes beyond the physical – interfaces designed to coerce users into making poor choices for them, or where the system is fundamentally biased (such as some AI systems) were all specified, developed and deployed by technologists. This book is for the people in the thick of it – coders, system architects, project managers, consultants – trying to do their jobs well in an environment where 'working code' may no longer be enough. Increasingly, success isn't just measured in development time, uptime and throughput – it's about the impact and consequences of these high-stake systems.

We won't drown you in ethics theory. But we will offer practical tools: questions you can ask, frameworks you can use, patterns to recognise. We'll explore some real-world cases – from headline scandals to daily dilemmas – to illustrate what acting ethically really looks like when deadlines loom and expectations rise.

But we won't stop at what went wrong. This book also identifies models, tools and questions to guide more ethical practice across the tech ecosystem: from individual decision making to organisational culture, from sustainability to emerging technology. You'll find accessible frameworks rooted in real-world dilemmas, not abstract idealism.

Our goal is not to preach, but to equip – to provide a flexible reference that supports professional development, helps meet industry codes of conduct (such as those upheld by BCS), and, ultimately, helps foster a computing culture grounded in trust, transparency and respect for human dignity. Ethics isn't an add-on to tech work. It's at its heart. While some texts explore ethical theory or case law, this book bridges the gap with hands-on strategies designed for daily use across the tech lifecycle – from ideation to retirement – helping organisations and individuals embed ethics where it matters most: in practice. Welcome to your practical guide to doing it better.

The following chapters in this book are structured to provide an exploration of issues of tech ethics. Chapter 2 explains the concept of tech ethics itself, providing a brief outline of some of the ethical philosophies and principles, and why these matter to individual professionals and to organisations. Chapter 3 delves into this individual perspective, and then in Chapter 4 we explore the organisational context and issues. Chapter 5 looks at the broader societal environment, with the impact of technology on the surrounding society. In Chapter 6, we explore the world impact of technology, and how global challenges can help to frame and focus what we do as technology professionals. Chapter 7 reflects on the emerging ethical challenges that new technologies, such as AI, are creating. We close in Chapter 8 looking forward to the future of tech ethics, and some of the individual opportunities for you, the reader, to develop your own professional expertise in this critical domain, with models, tools and resources that can aid in facing some of the difficult decisions we have to make, to ensure that IT is truly good for society.

2 FOUNDATIONS OF TECH ETHICS

Bernd Carsten Stahl

Having established the overall aims and context in the introduction, in this chapter we define tech ethics by unpacking both technology as a human-driven system and ethics as a layered framework of norms and values. We introduce three major ethical theories – consequentialism, deontology and virtue ethics – using relatable tech scenarios. We then categorise ethical issues into three types: immediate harms from tech artefacts, broader societal impacts and deeper metaphysical questions. Finally, we explore the role of professionals within a complex tech ecosystem, highlighting their responsibility to lead ethical practice through informed, context-aware decisions.

THE NEED FOR CONCEPTUAL CLARITY

In the introduction we encountered some high-profile examples of ethical concerns. It probably does not require much persuasion to recognise them as ethical issues. While such intuitive recognition is important and much public debate is based on it, a more fine-grained definition and delineation of the concept of tech ethics is needed for technologists. We need this to ensure consistency throughout the book but, more broadly, to underpin intellectual rigour when approaching, discussing and addressing tech ethics questions. The readers of a book on professional issues are likely to be more interested in practical insights and proposals than in a conceptual analysis, but we should still take the time to ensure that the basic concepts are clear. This should furthermore resonate with IT professionals who recognise the importance of attention to detail and clear definitions.

THE CONCEPT OF TECH ETHICS

It is useful to briefly look at the two components of the term tech ethics – at 'tech' and 'ethics' – before we explore what constitutes tech ethics.

What is tech?

The term technology, for which 'tech' is an abbreviated form, has its origin in the Greek *tekhnē* which stands for art, skill, craft in work; a system or method of making or doing[1]. The ending 'logy' points to the systematisation of the related knowledge in a theory or science. This indicates that a technology is a human way of interacting with the external environment by making something in a structured manner. Technology typically makes and uses tools and is often associated with the application of science in doing so. It is important to recognise that this is not just a general view of technology as a concept, but this concept is typically seen as part of what makes us humans, that technology use sets humans apart from other animals (Weizenbaum, 1977). There is a long tradition of seeing humans as tool users and, notwithstanding the fact that other animals have been recognised as using tools, the way that human life and civilisation relies on intricate tools turns them into defining features of entire civilisations (Arendt, 1958).

When we use the term 'tech' in this book, we do not cover all technologies that are available to humanity, but we tend to focus on information technology as the subset of technologies that are used to collect, process, analyse and display (digital) data. In the early days of computing such information technology was easy to recognise, as it took the form of mainframe and later personal computers. Ever since

---

1 etymonline.com/word/technology

computing devices started to shrink to the point where they powered mobile devices and were integrated into all sorts of artefacts, it has become more difficult to draw the line between information technology and other technology. It has been remarked that the differences between technologies and families of technologies are becoming increasingly blurry, which has led to the coining of the term 'converging technology' (Coenen and Simakova, 2013; Grunwald, 2013; Helbing and Ienca, 2024) which, in addition to information technology, can cover fields like neurotechnology, cognitive technology, nanotechnology and others. For the purposes of this book, we include any device or expression of technology that contributes to the processing of digital data in the 'tech' concept.

A final point on tech worth noting is that it never appears on its own and without human intervention. All tech is part of so-called socio-technical systems (Avgerou and McGrath, 2007; Beekman and Mumford, 1994), which means that it is created by humans for specific purposes, and that it has consequences and implications for human beings. Ethical questions are typically related to the overall socio-technical system and are rarely if ever an exclusive consequence of the artefact. On the one hand this is an obvious observation. On the other hand, it sometimes gets overlooked in ethics-oriented discussions which points to the importance of defining the term 'ethics' as well.

What is ethics?

Just like technology, the term 'ethics' has its root in Greek, stemming from *ēthos* which means custom or character. Since the late middle ages the term has been used to refer to moral principles, or the 'science of morals'[2]. The term 'ethics' is widely used in the English language and is familiar to most speakers. This familiarity masks the fact that the term can refer to fundamentally different phenomena. All of these have to do with questions of good and bad, right and wrong,

---

2 etymonline.com/word/ethic

acceptable and unacceptable. But they are still relatively easy to distinguish.

Elsewhere (Stahl, 2012) we have suggested a distinction of four different ways of using the term ethics. On the most basic level, we speak of ethics when we refer to what we know to be right and wrong, which guides our everyday behaviour, and which we rarely question. In this sense it is ethical to make way for others, say good morning when coming into the office, not offend friends etc. We make numerous decisions every day based on this implicit knowledge of ethics. This aspect of ethics is indivisibly aligned with customs and culture and provides the backbone of acceptable interaction. We all learn this when we grow up, when we get socialised into our groups and organisations, and continue to hone it throughout our lives.

On occasion this basic level of ethics fails. This may be when we do something that we find to be acceptable, but others don't or when we encounter new situations where our existing repertoire of ethical rules is not clearly applicable. This is the point where implicit ethics needs to be explicitly formulated. This can take the form of general rules that we think should be followed, such as 'you should respect other people's intellectual property' or 'one should not offend others online'. Making such rules explicit can help us understand our positions and, where there is disagreement, clarify the basis of this disagreement.

There are cases where such explicit normative statements, such as statements that tell us to behave in certain ways, conflict, contradict each other or are incompatible. An example could be the already cited rule 'one should not offend others online', which may conflict with a rule like 'one should be allowed to say whatever one wishes to say'. When we encounter such contradictory norms, we need to take recourse to an independent position that allows an analysis of the foundations and justifications of such norms and thereby facilitates the comparison between them. This is the role of ethics in the sense of moral philosophy.

Moral philosophy has been a formal part of the philosophical discourse for at least two and a half millennia and forms part of all philosophical systems. The practice of finding justifications for norms is probably much older and forms part of the nature of humanity. In the European context, much of the discourse of moral philosophy can be traced back to Greek antiquity. There are numerous ethical theories and positions. In current tech ethics one can find frequent references to three distinct theoretical positions: deontology, teleology and virtue ethics (Gal et al., 2022). Deontology, derived from the Greek word for 'duty', holds that the ethical quality of an action can be assessed by exploring the intention or maxim of the agent. The German philosopher Immanuel Kant thought that the only good thing is the good will, and this is good when it is informed by duty (Kant, 1797). A completely different approach is proposed by teleology, derived from the Greek word for 'end' that holds that the ethical evaluation of an action should focus on the consequences of that action, an idea famously developed by utilitarian scholars (Bentham, 1789; Mill, 1861). Virtue ethics, finally, looks to the character of the agent to determine what should count as good or bad, a position typically linked to Aristotle (2007).

Three views of ethics

Ethical theory can feel abstract – until you're in a meeting deciding whether to track users, retain data or prioritise speed over fairness. Suppose you are asked to implement a detailed user tracking feature to improve product recommendations – even if users aren't clearly informed. The ethical approaches can help in exploring the issues.

- **Teleological (consequentialist)**: *Is this the best outcome overall?*

Here an argument could be that 'If the tracking improves user satisfaction, boosts engagement and helps the business thrive, then it's a net positive'. However...

- **Deontological (duty-based)**: *Does this action respect ethical principles, regardless of the consequences?*

From this perspective you could argue that 'Users have a right to know what data we collect. Skipping informed consent, even with good intentions, violates that duty'. And finally...

- **Virtue ethics (character-based)**: *What would a good, trustworthy developer do?*

With this perspective, it could be said that 'Someone acting with integrity and respect for users would not do this without their knowledge'. Here, the ethical path is the one that reflects honesty, transparency and care.

These ethical views can lead to quite different outcomes. Of course, the wider context – with professional duties and legal requirements around data protection – would align with the second and third perspectives.

While this chapter focuses on widely taught Western traditions, there are other ethical traditions grounded in different parts of the world, sometimes linked to or arising out of different religious or cultural perspectives. Approaches like care ethics, which emphasise relational responsibility, and non-Western traditions such as Ubuntu or Confucianism, offer alternative ways to think about harm, obligation and justice. These perspectives can offer valuable insights – especially in global, cross-cultural tech contexts. However, this book is not a philosophical treatise, and we can leave the introduction to philosophical ethics here. It is important for a tech professional to understand, however, that questions of ethics not only have a very long history that much predates modern technologies, but also that it is rarely clear cut. An ethical analysis of a specific issue may include many different arguments from different perspectives that can, but often don't, lead to agreement and consensus. It is the nature of ethics that it deals with dilemmas, with situations where there is not one clearly identifiable right course of action but with decisions under uncertainty and with limited information where there are good arguments for different, sometimes contradictory positions. These ethical discussions take place in societies where ethical questions can intersect and are often influenced by other types of arguments, such as political, economic or legal ones.

Ethics, even though it is fundamentally concerned with the question of what is right and what is wrong, will only in rare circumstances be able to answer such questions unambiguously.

WHAT ARE ETHICAL ISSUES OF TECHNOLOGY?

There is much debate on ethics in tech which makes use of the three ethical positions just briefly introduced or other theoretical positions that we don't have the space to introduce here. This happens in discussions of computer ethics (Bynum, 2010), information ethics (Floridi, 2010), digital ethics (Floridi, 2019), AI ethics (Coeckelbergh, 2020) and related fields. We would encourage tech professionals to engage with these discussions, as they have an important contribution to make to them.

However, in professional and societal practice, there is often insufficient time and background to unpack the intricacies required for a full-blown ethical analysis. In practice, much of the debate revolves around what one can call 'ethical issues'. These are often high-profile instances where digital artefacts are involved in circumstances that are broadly recognised as being ethically problematic. This is typically the case where technology inflicts or threatens harms on individuals or groups. This can include the infringement of rights, in particular fundamental or human rights as expressed in the Universal Declaration of Human Rights (United Nations, 1948) or the European Convention on Human Rights (Council of Europe, 1950). It often includes harms that are already subject to legislation and regulation (e.g. discrimination, harassment), but can also cover harms that sit outside formal regulatory frameworks (e.g. change to social relationships, effects on employment structures).

The number of such ethical issues of tech is potentially infinite and they can change rapidly, depending on progress and capabilities of current technical artefacts. However, while there may be many specific ethical issues, there seems to be a set of categories of such issues that are fairly stable over time (Stahl et al., 2016). In a discussion of the ethics of AI we have suggested a three-part categorisation that we believe to be relevant to digital technologies more broadly: specific issues related to a technical artefact, general questions about living in a digital world and broader metaphysical questions (Stahl, 2021).

Specific issues related to a technical artefact are those where immediate harms to human beings are linked to specific technology uses. Given the nature of digital technologies, many of those are linked to data privacy and data protection which, if violated, can lead to discrimination, biases, financial losses and many other harms. Such immediate threats are often linked to protection of data and systems from illegitimate access and use. Some of these issues may be subject to technical fixes and resolutions.

General questions about living in a technical world are those issues that arise due to or linked with digital tech and typically have broader social and societal connotations. Examples of such issues include the following:

- With the distribution of resources and power, tech has the potential to lead to radically new economic models and distributions. In practice, this impact seems to have had the effect of concentrating wealth in a small number of tech firms (Zuboff, 2019).

- This concentration of wealth and power can spawn a vicious circle where increasing profits provide the basis for the development of technologies that further strengthen the big companies. Given the geo-political concentration of some of the major companies, this shows why tech ethics needs to address the issue of control, benefits and impact.

- Other examples of social consequences can be observed in the political sphere where technology can skew or even undermine elections and democratic processes, for example by voter manipulation (see the example of the Facebook/Cambridge Analytica case (Berghel, 2018)). Deep fakes may influence democratic decisions and be used to unfairly promote specific political positions.

- A related issue can arise where automated decisions are made by IT systems. GDPR/UK GDPR allow for people to request review of such decisions, but there is the issue of whether these decisions are clear to customers and whether they understand their rights.

- A further example of a society-level concern is in the area of the military. Novel technologies, in particular those based on growing levels of autonomy, not only have the potential to shape the way wars are conducted, but also when and how wars are started. At the time of writing this chapter (July 2025) we can observe an international pivot towards more emphasis on military and defence with the UK pledging to spend five per cent of GDP on the military. Significant amounts of these investments will go into military AI and other digital technologies thus heightening the need for ethical reflection and scrutiny.

These types of issues are not subject to technical resolution, but form part of broader social and political debates and decisions.

The final set of ethical issues are those that can be called metaphysical because they relate to our views of the fundamental nature of reality. These relate to questions such as whether machines can be conscious, whether they can have true autonomy and whether they may surpass humans in meaningful ways and maybe even replace us. These questions are linked to terms like transhumanism (Livingstone, 2015), the singularity (Kurzweil, 2006) or superintelligence (Bostrom,

2016). These questions relate to how we see the role of humans in the world and what our relationship to the technology can, will or should be. Some of these questions may not be subject to resolution at all but may remain on a conceptual level.

HOW CAN WE RESOLVE ETHICAL ISSUES? PROFESSIONALISM IN CONTEXT

Ethical issues and ethical theories stand in a complex relationship. Ethical theory certainly does not offer clear-cut solutions to ethical issues. But theory can help better understand the issues and explore how they are framed, which presuppositions they contain, and which ways of dealing with them may be preferable over others.

To a large extent ethical issues will not be subject to simple resolution. Unlike a technical challenge where an optimum solution may be possible, in the case of ethical issues the problem itself tends to be multi-faceted, the selection of ways of addressing them based on often implicit beliefs and the outcomes will remain subject to discussion. This points back to the dilemma nature of ethics which rarely allows for a universally accepted solution.

However, the fact that ethical issues cannot be resolved does not mean that we can either ignore them or follow the path of least resistance. The various issues listed above do exist and as a society we need to deal with them to the best of our abilities. There is an array of responses to ethical issues that a society can put forward. These range from the soft, such as societal disapproval of certain actions leading to public expressions of disagreement, to stronger policy-level responses all the way to the criminalisation of actions we find abhorrent.

Responses to ethical issues are not the sole preserve of society and the state. They can inform activities of organisations and networks that can develop policies, principles and standards. There are types of organisations that have a specific role to play, such as schools, universities and other educational organisations. The media play an important role in forming opinions and facilitating debates. Standardisation bodies can pick up agreements and formalise them. Part of the response will also be individual, where an individual can form their opinion on which technology to use or refuse to use, which purposes to use it for and where to draw the boundaries.

Overall, it may be helpful to use the metaphor of an ecosystem to think about the ethics of tech. Rather than assume that there are specific issues caused by clearly defined technologies or applications that have easily identifiable solutions, one can think about ethical questions as distributed across an ecosystem consisting of individuals, groups, organisations, technologies and their environment. An example might be a (semi) autonomous uncrewed aerial vehicle. In and of itself such a UAV has an infinity of uses that are difficult to predict and evaluate. However, within a military ecosystem, the UAV may have specific capability for surveillance or attack, may be geared towards specific rules of engagement, and provide new capabilities that significantly change tactical and even strategic options for commanders. Such a UAV can also be imagined within a logistics ecosystem where it might be optimised for delivery, providing new options for time-critical deliveries, for example of blood packs, but also changing the nature of commodity ordering of online shopping.

Interfering with such an ecosystem may address some questions in part of the ecosystem but may have unpredicted consequences in unexpected parts of the ecosystem. This system-level interaction and complexity is worth keeping in mind when thinking about tech ethics. In Chapter 4 we build on the ecosystem model, illustrating how organisational factors – such as leadership culture and incentive structures – interact with regulatory, legal and individual-level influences to shape ethical decision making.

Professional bodies and their individual members in their roles as professionals have an important role to play in this ecosystem context. Professional bodies can contribute to the development of strategies, policies and standards that drive individual and collective action. Individual professionals have crucial roles across private sector, governmental and non-profit organisations involved in the development and use of tech. They can adopt, build on and amplify current agreements on good practice. Professionals and their organisations are by no means the only stakeholders in this context, but they have a privileged position as technical experts and holders of a trusted status that puts demands on them to bring to bear not just their technical expertise, but also their understanding of the organisational and societal impact of tech, and they can lead by example in dealing with ethical and social issues linked to tech. The next chapter explores professional ethics, with later chapters illustrating the organisational and broader context of tech ethics.

REFERENCES

Arendt, H. (1958) *The Human Condition: Second Edition*. Chicago, IL, USA: University of Chicago Press.

Aristotle. (2007) *The Nicomachean Ethics*. Minneapolis, MN, USA: Filiquarian Publishing, LLC.

Avgerou, C. and McGrath, K. (2007) 'Power, rationality, and the art of living through socio-technical change'. *MIS Quarterly*, 31 (2). 95–315.

Beekman, G.J. and Mumford, E. (1994) *Tools for Change and Progress: A Socio-Technical Approach to Business Process Re-Engineering*. Leiden, Netherlands: CSG Publications.

Bentham, J. (1789) *An Introduction to the Principles of Morals and Legislation*. Mineola, NY, USA: Dover Publications Inc.

Berghel, H. (2018) 'Malice domestic: The Cambridge analytica dystopia'. *Computer*. IEEE Computer Society, 51 (05). 84–89.

Bostrom, N. (2016) *Superintelligence: Paths, Dangers, Strategies*. Reprint edition. Oxford, UK; New York, NY, USA: Oxford University Press.

Bynum, T.W. (2010) The historical roots of information and computer ethics. In: Floridi, L. (ed.) *The Cambridge Handbook of*

Information and Computer Ethics. Cambridge, UK: Cambridge University Press. 20–38.

Coeckelbergh, M. (2020) *AI Ethics*. Cambridge, MA, USA: The MIT Press.

Coenen, C. and Simakova, E. (2013) 'STS policy interactions, technology assessment and the governance of technovisionary sciences'. *Science, Technology & Innovation Studies*, 9 (2). 3–20.

Council of Europe. (1950) *European Convention on Human Rights*.

Floridi, L. (2010) Information ethics. In: Floridi, L. (ed.) *The Cambridge Handbook of Information and Computer Ethics*. Cambridge, UK: Cambridge University Press. 77–97.

Floridi, L. (2019) 'Translating principles into practices of digital ethics: Five risks of being unethical'. *Philosophy & Technology*, 32. 185–193. Available from doi.org/10.1007/s13347-019-00354-x.

Gal, U., Hansen, S. and Lee, A. (2022) 'Research perspectives: toward theoretical rigor in ethical analysis: The case of algorithmic decision-making systems'. *Journal of the Association for Information Systems*, 23 (6). 1634–1661. doi: 10.17705/1jais.00784.

Grunwald, A. (2013) 'Techno-visionary sciences: Challenges to policy advice'. *Science, Technology & Innovation Studies*, 9 (2). 21–38.

Helbing, D. and Ienca, M. (2024) 'Why converging technologies need converging international regulation'. *Ethics and Information Technology*, 26 (1). 15. doi: 10.1007/s10676-024-09756-8.

Kant, I. (1797) *Grundlegung Zur Metaphysik Der Sitten*. Ditzingen, Germany: Reclam.

Kurzweil, R. (2006) *The Singularity Is Near*. London, UK: Gerald Duckworth & Co Ltd.

Livingstone, D. (2015) *Transhumanism: The History of a Dangerous Idea*. Scotts Valley, CA, USA: CreateSpace Independent Publishing Platform.

Mill, J.S. (1861) *Utilitarianism.* Second revised edition. Indianapolis, IN, USA: Hackett Publishing Co, Inc.

Stahl, B.C. (2012) 'Morality, ethics, and reflection: A categorization of normative IS research'. *Journal of the Association for Information Systems*, 13 (8). 636–656. doi: 10.17705/1jais.00304.

Stahl, B.C. (2021) *Artificial Intelligence for a Better Future: An Ecosystem Perspective on the Ethics of AI and Emerging Digital Technologies.* Cham, Switzerland: Springer International Publishing. doi: 10.1007/978-3-030-69978-9.

Stahl, B.C., Timmermans, J. and Mittelstadt, B.D. (2016) 'The ethics of computing: A survey of the computing-oriented literature'. *ACM Computing Surveys*, 48 (4). 55:1–55:38. doi: 10.1145/2871196.

United Nations. (1948) *Universal Declaration of Human Rights.*

Weizenbaum, J. (1977) *Computer Power and Human Reason: From Judgement to Calculation.* New edition. San Francisco, CA, USA: W.H. Freeman & Co Ltd.

Zuboff, S. (2019) *The Age of Surveillance Capitalism: The Fight for a Human Future at the New Frontier of Power.* First edition. London, UK: Profile Books.

3 THE PROFESSIONAL INDIVIDUAL'S ETHICS

Darren Dalcher

Given the ethical concepts defined in Chapter 2, we now explore professional ethics as a vital tool and framework to navigate moral complexity in tech and innovation. We consider how the competing value systems – personal, organisational, societal – are influenced by practical issues such as deadlines, politics and self-interest. We suggest practical tools and reflective questions to help individuals and teams reason through dilemmas, act responsibly and build ethical competence. The chapter also examines different types of responsibility – causal, legal, moral and role-based – and presents codes of conduct as scaffolding for professional integrity.

WHAT ARE PROFESSIONAL ETHICS AND HOW TO MANAGE THEM

In an increasingly uncertain and contested world, ethics plays a crucial role in enabling professionals to conduct their affairs, make decisions and interact with others. This chapter endeavours to provide managers and developers with the vocabulary, practical tools and frameworks needed to address ethical and moral challenges in a professional setting. The chapter identifies the practical importance of ethics, before offering a snapshot of ethical challenges and attitudes and presenting some of the key pressures on professionals. It introduces ethics as a clash of value systems leading to ethical dilemmas and offers frameworks and tools for considering and utilising ethics at the personal, collective and professional levels. The concept of responsibility is introduced as a lens for developing professional practice, before highlighting a multiplicity of types of responsibility and presenting a professional code of ethics that can be applied in organisations seeking to develop moral and ethical capability. The approach thus positions professional ethics as a critical ingredient in avoiding moral hazards and securing enduring success and sustainability.

ETHICS IN PROFESSIONAL PRACTICE

The area of ethics is assuming greater importance in tech and innovation with most professional associations establishing their own codes of conduct. Indeed, in an era of professionalisation and reflection there is an implicit expectation that developers and engineers will behave in an ethical way and discharge their duties in a moral and responsible fashion. Many of the codes stipulate that potential breaches may result in exclusion or further sanctions, suggesting that there is a clear position that can be evaluated and judged by an external agency. In reality, with the exception of the most obvious and unprofessional practices, this is likely to prove challenging as will be shown in this chapter.

Published codes of ethics require individuals to follow standards of professional ethics and behave 'appropriately'. They broadly explain that professionals need to act in equity, good faith and good conscience with due regard for the interests of the organisation or client. Ethical requirements form an integral part of professional behaviour and require fundamental understanding of expectations, moral values and legal boundaries, thereby necessitating developers and managers to display morally, legally and socially appropriate manners of behaving and working. The implication is that practitioners require both knowledge and competence related to ethics and its application within the working context.

Ethics is considered to be essential to free enterprise, democracy and the functioning of a fair society. Yet, despite the good intentions, the establishment of ethical thinking and reflection in practice seems a long way off. There are a number of primary challenges that impinge on the application of ethics in practice:

- **Practicality**: Establishing ethics as a valid practical concern that extends beyond theoretical moralising. Professionals require practical tools, approaches, thinking frames and ways of applying them to their own contexts rather than generalised philosophical positioning and preaching.

- **Complexity**: Recognising the complexity of ethical settings. Overly simplistic depictions of ethics as a choice between **right vs wrong** need to be replaced by more nuanced understanding of multidimensional dilemmas and conflicting sets of choices.

- **Pressure**: Acknowledging and addressing organisational realities and politics. Individual decision makers do not operate in a vacuum. Even in situations where the right course of action is somewhat obvious, constraints related to business competitiveness, institutional pressures, political concerns, internal priorities, conflicts of interests and even personal gains and future promotions and remuneration may be applied and promoted by various parties.

- **Courage**: Developing moral courage and conviction. Against the backdrop of a moral decline and a series of ethical and financial scandals (including Enron, Bernard Madoff, VW emissions scandal), it might prove essential to develop personal moral courage as a way of combatting the so-called **ethics recession** and overcoming organisational and urgent technical, managerial and project-related pressures.

- **Guidance**: Moral action is not automatic. Knowing that a situation is not right does not offer an obvious course of resolution. Guidance and practical tools and frameworks are needed to support deliberation, resolution and action.

The following sections offer the vocabulary and thinking tools required to address the challenges, reason about ethical dilemmas, and develop a professional responsibility and the practical tools to address ethical concerns in technical settings.

DO WE HAVE A PROBLEM WITH ETHICS?

A 2018 survey conducted by the Institute of Business Ethics (IBE, 2018) in eight European countries revealed that 78 per cent of employees said that their organisation always or frequently acts with honesty. The values range between 69 per cent in Germany to 88 per cent in Ireland. Employees seemed more likely to speak up about misconduct with 54 per cent recorded overall, ranging from 67 per cent in the UK to 49 per cent in Portugal. However, one in three employees have been aware of misconduct at work, with 46 per cent recognising that people have been treated unethically, 35 per cent misrepresenting hours worked and 30 per cent reporting safety violations. Pressure on workers is also intensifying: 16 per cent of respondents across Europe have felt some form of pressure to compromise their organisation's ethical standard, with the figure rising in every country. Conversely, just under a quarter of participants (23 per cent) have felt incentivised to act ethically. Moreover, a 2021 survey with 10,000 respondents indicated that 43 per cent of people who spoke about ethics lapses and misconduct at work experienced retaliation as a result.

The 2020 Global Business Ethics survey reported similar trends and insights for the US and globally. The pressure to compromise ethical standards was the highest it has been throughout 20 years of surveys, with 29 per cent of respondents reporting pressure. Observed incidents of misconduct were on the rise. In the US, 80 per cent of respondents reported observed misconduct or unethical behaviour (ECI, 2020). However, 79 per cent of US employees and 61 per cent of global employees also reported experiencing retaliation for raising ethical concerns. In 2016 the greatest pressure to compromise standards was reported by respondents from Brazil, India and Russia (ECI, 2016).

The top ten reasons and justifications given for the pressure to act unethically in a 2024 Ethics at Work survey conducted across sixteen countries with over 12,000 participants (IBE, 2024) will feel familiar to many developers and managers (listed in order):

- I was following my boss's orders.
- There was time pressure or an unrealistic deadline.
- I felt peer pressure to be a team player.
- I was being asked to take shortcuts.
- I was trying to save my job.
- We were under-resourced.
- I had to meet unrealistic business objectives or deadlines.
- I wanted to help the organisation perform better.
- There were financial or budgeting pressures at the company.
- My organisation has an unethical culture.

Indeed, the pressure of a delivering to a strict deadline on a short-term intensive project with unrealistic objectives and deadlines in an intense team setting may resonate with many imperatives observed within the specific context of tech and innovation projects. If ethics is concerned with making good decisions regarding people, resources, objectives and the environment, attention to ethics is particularly important in times of change and transformation, which is when the temptation to rush ahead and cut corners may be at its highest.

Ethics raises interesting questions regarding priorities, pressure and power. Explaining the host of reasons for pressure as listed above and the concerns regarding speaking about misconduct and ethical lapses invokes the need to introduce a further **prudential** dimension concerned with self-interest. Prudential reasons relate to the personal interest of the decision maker which could be described in terms of personal financial gains, or some other pertinent values such as fairness, justice, loyalty, honesty, openness, integrity, accountability, kindness, charity, friendliness or trustworthiness. Prudential considerations would necessitate balancing issues, trading off values and reaching difficult compromises between competing personal priorities and unethical concerns, which may result in increased pressure and anxiety for managers, leaders and other participants. Many ethical dilemmas embody such prudential elements, making the ethical vs. prudential trade-offs both personal and problematic. Ironically, even the decision to speak up about unethical concerns and lapses involves a balance between ethical considerations and a recognition of potential prudential harm to the informant, their interests or their community.

ETHICS AS A CLASH OF SYSTEMS

Many books and commentators position ethics as the choice between right and wrong, often relating it to fairness or to some kind of acceptable standards for human behaviour and conduct. Indeed, it would be reassuring to be able to reduce ethical conflict and professional decisions to rights and wrongs; however, this is an overly simplistic representation of ethics offering the wrong starting point. Right versus wrong situations imply a relatively straightforward resolution, a choice between black and white. Ethics becomes more arduous when we encounter grey areas, where managers have to choose between right and right as conflicting perspectives and different shades of grey come into play. Ethics is also invoked in situations where the right course of action is somewhat obvious, but constraints related to business competitiveness, institutional pressures, political concerns, internal priorities, conflicts of interests and even personal gains and promotions may be applied by various parties.

The basis for ethics is the focus on values held by different individuals and groups and the ability to reconcile different sets of beliefs. Values emerge from fundamental beliefs. Managers will have different sets of beliefs derived from their personal background, upbringing, education, training and experiences. They can thus accumulate personal, team, organisational, professional, sector-related, national, societal and human values. They will also be expected to gain an understanding of the values relevant to their clients, users and stakeholder communities, which may originate from a variety of backgrounds. More complex trade-offs, such as the triple bottom line, where financial, environmental and social perspectives are combined, require even more sensitive ways of balancing contrasting values and preferences.

Ethical dilemmas are problematic because they represent a clash between right and right (or sometimes between wrong and wrong), implying a direct conflict between competing moral requirements. For instance, how do we choose between being a good parent and a good employee? The existence of moral pluralism is problematic precisely because it eliminates the judgment between right and wrong as the deciding criterion, introducing a need for demarcating different aspects and shades of goodness, developing grading structures for determining preferential or better fits, or establishing who should suffer more and over what time.

Ethical decision making is about grappling with conflicting values from different thinking systems and perspectives rather than undisputable scientific facts. Dilemmas imply that neither of the propositions is unambiguously and universally preferable, mandating a new capability for dealing with competing and even opposing moral positions, rules and criteria.

The objective is to make informed, good enough decisions. Ethical responsibility is therefore concerned with how we behave and how things are done within our personal, collective and professional realms, freedoms and limits. In the course of taking action, we strive not to compromise the interests of the project, the involved parties, the participating organisations, society and the wider environment, whilst upholding our own personal values, addressing our innate sense of fairness and considering the common good.

PERSONAL ETHICS: WHAT IS THE RIGHT THING TO DO?

Ethical behaviour does not simply emerge from having a professional code of conduct, a series of workshops, a neat form or a departmental ethics committee. Ethical behaviour starts with individuals who are willing to engage and grapple with their personal values, social or communal assumptions, choices and decisions. Individuals endeavour to balance their own levels of discomfort in a given situation with their internal values, whilst taking into consideration the prudential dimension and the potential for personal impact. Not surprisingly, unpacking the set of questions required to make sense of a situation can be difficult and many managers lament the lack of concrete suggestions to explore whilst engaging with ethical dilemmas. The following set offers a simplified framework for engaging with ethical concerns and developing a moral and ethical competence.

1. Is it legal?

The first question is occasionally positioned by some organisations as the lowest bar, established by focusing on what the law requires, expects or permits. The aim of the question is to consider the existing standards, as ethics and the law are often intertwined, but ethics can also be used to augment, refresh and strengthen legislative and governance scrutiny. The ethical features of a situation are frequently contrasted with legal aspects, representing a minimal standard. However, the law creates structures within which rules and codes are intended to operate. Murder, assault and drug taking may be illegal in most jurisdictions, whilst paying tax is an obligation in most, albeit not all, domains. Legislation is unlikely to be sufficiently comprehensive to address all potential circumstances and conceivable human actions. Moreover, legal standards are reactive, often induced by significant ethical lapses. It may take years to catch up and become enshrined as statues, laws and legislative standards, as exemplified by the delays in creating laws prohibiting slavery and bribery. This is particularly applicable in the case of new technologies and novel applications that may raise ethical concerns long before they mature into fully formed legislative criteria. What is legal is not necessarily ethical, whilst what is not illegal is not necessarily moral. Ethics generally extends beyond the regulatory dictates of the legal system into the discretionary world of fairness, honesty, trust, responsibility and choice, thereby enabling additional tests and enhanced standards of behaviour to be introduced. In the language of the ethical theories described in the first chapter, this question has a deontological feel to it: is there a rule or maxim that governs the decision?

2. Is it fair?

The second question probes the integrity and fairness aspects by addressing concerns through sub-questions such as: Is it right? Is it balanced? Am I hurting anyone? Who will be affected by it? Is it fair to all concerned parties?

This set of questions looks at who might be favoured by the action (or lack thereof) immediately and over the long term. It identifies affected parties and potential stakeholders and looks at the implications of taking action, as well as leaving things as they are. Win-win scenarios may be difficult to construct, but understanding the potential winners and losers amongst stakeholders helps to clarify levels of power, resistance and resentment and map potential future conflicts. Imbalances tend to hamper future relationships and hinder the potential for sustainable success and prosperity. With reference to the first chapter, this set of reflections has a teleological edge; how are we maximising the good of all parties or minimising harms to them?

3. How will I feel afterwards?

Ethics is personal. The third question returns to the ethical dilemma and the feelings and emotions it engenders. It examines the position and role of the decision maker, encouraging scrutiny of their ethical values and priorities, their sense of morality, their emotions, their standards, their prudential concerns, their willingness to engage and their readiness to take remedial action or potentially to report an injustice. It encourages decision makers to take ownership for the decision they make or fail to take. It can also give managers the courage to ask brave questions, seek answers, raise concerns and report ethical breaches. Additional sub-questions may include:

- Can I live with this situation?
- Can I look at myself in the mirror afterwards?
- Will it make me feel proud?
- Can I afford to ignore it?
- Will it keep me awake at night?

4. Can I really justify it?

Some deliberations are tougher than others. The final set of heavy-duty questions and considerations requires deeper engagement with the scenario through the use of more sophisticated and emotional questions:

- First of all, put yourself in the other person's shoes – will the affected person also think that the decision is ethical?
- How would I like it if it happened to my daughter, partner, father, grandmother?
- How would I explain the decision to my (future) children?
- How would my mother feel about my decision if she were to hear about it in the shop or read about it in a newspaper?

These last two sets of personal questions are closely related to the concept of virtue ethics introduced in Chapter 1. In essence these questions are asking what a good/virtuous person would do in this situation.

COLLECTIVE ETHICS: PULLING PEOPLE TOGETHER

Groups, teams and communities play an ever-increasing role in the workplace. Projects bring together temporary groups of engineers, developers and managers, collections of stakeholders and specific interest groups, whilst creating new communities of users. Such endeavours rely on professionals to apply their own moral and ethical codes. Organisations often seek to engender an ethical culture; yet, while they may establish a moral identity, recruit individuals with moral sensitivity and awareness, and provide support and encouragement for ethical scrutiny, it is ultimately up to the individuals to choose to think ethically and act responsibly.

But what happens when many individuals only consider their own interests? Individualism seems to be a prevalent feature of modern life. The legal system specifies unacceptable behaviour in society for the good of all. Yet, well intended individual acts of freedom can accumulate and strain the entire community. Dalcher (2022) explores the implications of community life that requires cooperative co-existence and implied adherence to group patterns that focus on the long-term sustainability of a cherished resource and the community it supports. Moreover, even an individualistic and seemingly harmless action, such as hanging a lovelock on a bridge to signify an eternal commitment to a beloved partner, multiplied thousands of times over can lead to the collapse of a highly prized common resource or the destruction of a landmark. The ethics and realities of living and working in a community are bound together through the actions, infractions, priorities and morals of individual members.

Collective working requires long-term consideration of impacts and actions across and between groups. Yet, it also carries the benefit of enabling multiple independent ethical agents to collaborate, share and support one another. Organisations can play a part in motivating and encouraging communal ethical behaviour. Morality is developed and fine-tuned over time and can be encouraged to grow and develop. The main influencing behaviours in organisations stem from the establishment of culture, values, standards of behaviour and practices that support community co-existence, ethical behaviour and moral decision making. Blanchard and Peale (1988) formalised the 5Ps framework as the basis for developing an ethics policy and attitude offering a way of structuring an underpinning ethical perspective and an enduring matching attitude (re-labelled and paraphrased below):

- **Purpose**: A high calling. A combination of vision, values and shared meaning that helps to mould the expectations of acceptable and unacceptable behaviours.

- **Pride**: Healthy self-esteem. Healthy balance of dignity, self-respect and humility play a part in encouraging employees to act in an ethical manner. Pride also enables actors to resist the temptation to behave unethically.

- **Patience**: A question of faith. Patience requires commitment, long-term dedication and capacity to accept setbacks and having faith and belief that things will work out in the long run. Belief in long-term success encourages resilience in the face of obstacles and bad news, whilst sustaining a positive disposition and a long-term perspective.

- **Persistence**: Full time commitment. Perseverance and commitment to staying the course.

- **Perspective**: Seeing what is really important. The ability to step back, pause, reflect, take stock, see the big picture and understand what matters most in order to support the making of short-term as well as long-term decisions.

Ethical decisions are made by individuals. Nonetheless, the organisation, department or unit may also wish to review tech and project related dilemmas to evaluate their potential for harm and the impact on stakeholders, especially if the issues have been raised by employees, formally or informally. Specific new questions can build on the individual questions described above:

- Does the action/decision fit our values?

- Will it build goodwill?

- How would it look in the newspapers?
- Will it reflect poorly on our company?
- Will it cause long-term damage?

These concepts and how to deal with them in the specific context in which IT professionals work are discussed in the next chapter.

PROFESSIONAL ETHICS AND THE ROLE OF RESPONSIBILITY

Tech projects aim to solve problems or improve on a status quo; yet, their very emergence and their rushed implementation schedule open the potential for doing harm as well as good, especially when key stakeholders' needs and preferences are ignored. Ethics is an important source of guidance for decision making. Indeed, ethics as a set of values is expressed and given meaning through commitments, responsibilities and obligations. The values come into play when the boundaries between correct and incorrect behaviour are not clear, especially when multiple viewpoints and perspectives co-exist. According to the Institute for Business Ethics, business ethics is the application of ethical values to business behaviour. Tech development and deployment ethics could therefore be defined as the application of ethical values and principles to the deployment of technology and the management of appropriate projects, their outcomes and implications, whilst considering all involved parties and stakeholders.

Given that the responsibility for deploying tech, managing projects and overseeing their outcomes resides with developers, managers and sponsors, their ability to act independently and make decisions and their professional responsibility are crucial to understanding the role and impact of morality and ethics in this area. The Oxford English Dictionary defines 'responsible' as either 'liable to be called to account' or 'morally accountable for one's actions', thus encompassing two rather different interpretations. Nonetheless, the

31

increasing focus on the certification of developers, managers or engineers and the use of a chartered status standard carry significant implications in terms of assumed responsibility. Employing a professional represents the transfer of risk and decision-making obligations to a better-qualified agency, also known as transcendent responsibility. It carries within it the implicit assumptions of:

- trust in their ability and professional competence;
- security in the knowledge that a qualified expert is employed; and
- the comfort and peace of mind that come from this knowledge.

Professionals utilise specialised knowledge, skills, expertise and experience; established ways of thinking and working; professional or disciplinary norms; and legal and moral responsibility that can result in the satisfaction of a social purpose or societal need. Employing a professional in the role of a technical expert or trusted advisor is therefore akin to buying additional insurance (through a strategy of risk transfer). In return for the trust exhibited by the client, the professional developer or manager would undertake responsibility for the deployment of the agreed function, capability or quality, including the process and the product itself. This aspect of responsibility is subject to professionalism, morality and ethics. (The social obligations of professionalism are discussed more in Chapter 5.)

While responsibility entails owning up to acts, effects and consequences, one can identify distinctly different types of responsibility (Dalcher, 2007), as shown in Table 3.1.

Moral responsibility implies being answerable for one's actions and decisions and typically assumes some degree of causal responsibility. Therefore, a professional can also be held morally responsible for failing to act (re-setting the focus and scope of responsibility from harming to not aiding). Guilds, associations and professional bodies often look after

Table 3.1 Different types of responsibility

Causal responsibility	Associated with bringing something about either directly or indirectly (e.g. by ordering someone else).
Legal responsibility	Associated with fulfilling the requirements for accountability under the law.
Moral responsibility	Associated with having a moral obligation or fulfilling the criteria for deserving blame or praise for a morally significant act, or omission, and the resulting consequences.
Role responsibility	Associated with performing duties that are attached to particular professional or societal (or even biological) roles. Failure to fulfil such duties can expose the role-holder to moral, legal or constitutional censure.

the role responsibility aspect, thereby helping to enforce a more professional practice. Professional codes, introduced by such bodies, allow us to appreciate the standard, evaluate what could be expected from a member of the profession, and provide an implicit definition, at the very least, of acceptable professional behaviour. Indeed, with professional accreditation and certification, apportioning responsibilities may become a key activity in failure investigations.

DEVELOPING YOUR CODE OF ETHICS

The deployment of new technologies has always invoked questions regarding their potential harm and their impacts on humans, civil society and the wider environment. However, the rapid growth of tech, automation, artificial intelligence and machine learning is raising important new questions about the moral responsibilities associated with developing, managing and introducing such technologies.

Developers and managers have a responsibility to their profession and to wider society, in addition to their client and company. Developing a code for resolving dilemmas and making moral decisions by building on the preceding discussion can be useful in supporting the development of communal ethical reasoning and deliberation. A code of ethics comprises a set of ethical principles. It would therefore place several essential normative requirements on professional engineers and managers, including, as a minimum:

- an obligation to technical, managerial, leadership and moral competence, which may also entail personal and organisational recognition of gaps, shortfalls, limitations and lack of expertise, knowledge, capability or experience;

- an obligation to present and review evidence, theory and interpretation honestly, accurately and without bias and quantify all risks;

- an obligation and wider responsibility for timely communication of both positive and negative results;

- an obligation to voice concerns and speak truth to power in moral dilemmas;

- an acceptance of responsibility (causal, legal and moral) for actions, impacts and consequences;

- an obligation to limit the harms and ensure the safety of products, systems and outcomes and their effects on the environment; and

- an obligation to guard the interests of multiple participants and stakeholder groups.

Responsibility thus encompasses constant awareness, total autonomy and explicit accountability. The focus on accountability for consequences and outcomes of actions (or lack thereof) is essential in tech projects and innovation initiatives and can point to the potential for severe impact following deployment, during usage and beyond, extending into decommissioning and disposal and possibly supporting recycling and reuse options. It also recognises the impacts on others, including human, societal and environmental effects.

The penultimate clause encourages managers to ensure the public's safety and limit the potential harm to others. This is particularly important considering the experimental nature of every project and tech undertaking, the residual uncertainty that accompanies them, and the inability to predict and forecast all potential side effects and consequences (Martin and Schinzinger, 2010). If tech projects represent the ambition and the experiments of society, developers and managers thus become the responsible experimenters embracing a conscientious commitment to live by moral and ethical values required to safeguard society, the environment and all participants and stakeholders.

The BCS Code of Conduct builds on the above ideas, by emphasising four key duties and principles:

- Public interest – You make IT for everyone.
- Professional competence and integrity – Show what you know, learn what you don't.
- Duty to relevant authority – Respect the organisation or individual you work for.
- Duty to the profession – Keep IT real. Keep IT professional. Pass IT on.

Professional members who follow the code thus become ambassadors for the IT industry, using their voice and actions to make a positive difference to society.

CONCLUSION: MANAGING ETHICALLY

Invoking codes of ethics is not a new endeavour. Ancient societies have practised various ways of introducing such principles. One example is provided by Hammurabi, King of Babylon, who recognised the perils of design over 3,780 years ago and enacted a building code that clarified the 'responsibilities' of designers: 'If a builder has built a house for a man and his work is not strong, and if the house he has built falls and kills the householder, that builder shall be slain' – Code of Hammurabi, 1755 BC.

Professional societies are unlikely to introduce similar censure in the foreseeable future. They do however encourage members to consider the ethical and enduring implications of their decisions and actions. This should entail looking at the needs, assumptions and impacts across different groups and making decisions that are informed by the different concerns and preferences. Adopting a reflective practice that questions the assumptions and limitations of our approaches should be used by all practitioners interested in improving project success rates, delivering business value, and maintaining stakeholder relationships whilst preserving and sustaining the environment.

Ultimately, technology remains a human activity that defines and enables a new reality. Creating new IT systems and innovative services often implies designing and reconfiguring society and how it might operate. The choices made during such design will shape emerging possibilities and also determine who may be excluded from participation. Successful application requires IT professionals to extend beyond the technical issues and consider organisational, human and societal concerns, particularly when reflecting on issues of autonomy and agency. Over the past two decades we have become more comfortable with considerations of sustainability – as we come to terms with new technologies and their long-term impacts it would be encouraging to consider IT professionals as the stewards of inclusivity, and social and societal considerations.

Moral codes give individuals and communities the courage to act ethically. IT professionals are duty bound to update their knowledge, skills and attitudes. This may well include making sense of personal uncertainties and conflicts of opinion. Ethical issues become a concern when there are no written rules, when they raise moral problems for a member of the team, when they make managers reflect on what is right and when you are forced to consider where your obligations and duties lie (and probably when you are told that 'this is what you are being paid to do'). The role of ethical thinking is to safeguard practitioners, the profession and the stakeholders.

The outcomes of our tech deployment projects determine our progress towards a better and more comfortable future. Clients, users, stakeholders, employees and colleagues rely on the professionalism, responsibility and ethics of managers and developers in delivering that future responsibly. Who better to remind us of the need for professionalism than Astronaut Alan B. Shepard, who whilst awaiting blast-off atop the space shuttle Columbia, commented that it was a humbling experience knowing that his fate depended on a vehicle built by the lowest bidder.

A sobering food for thought for inventors, developers and managers, and another indication of the true complexity of responsibility, ethics and professionalism in technical projects.

Historically, ethics would only come to the forefront in the wake of significant disasters or scandals, raising questions regarding the use of flammable cladding materials in residential high-rise buildings, insufficient testing and lax governance in the space shuttle programme or the manipulation of emissions controls during car testing. Indeed, the combination of volatile new technologies, temporary setting, constant pressure, short deadlines, impending handover, multiple contractors, diverse participants and competitive pricing all add to the complexity and potential ethical vulnerabilities. However, there is a crucial need to use ethics as a force for identifying concerns, resolving issues and avoiding accidents, scandals or disasters. Professionals thus play an important part in raising awareness of impending moral hazards and in mitigating their potential effects, thereby adding to the risk, governance and assurance aspects of the project structure whilst contributing to the enduring success and sustainability of the endeavour.

The social, political, environmental and moral impacts of tech projects and their outcomes will continue to rise to match accelerating societal ambitions. To gain and retain trust, and enable communities to realise the benefits of these remarkable endeavours, managers will need to cultivate an ethical and professional dimension. Creating a fairer future for all would thus depend on our ability to confidently apply ethical tools, approaches and attitudes, such as the ones explored throughout this chapter, and to develop the determination to continue to ask courageous questions and speak truth to power, especially during the most trying and challenging times.

REFERENCES

Blanchard, K. and Peale, N. V. (1988) *The Power of Ethical Management*. New York, NY, USA: William Morrow and Company.

Dalcher, D. (2007) 'Why the pilot cannot be blamed: a cautionary note about excessive reliance on technology'. *International Journal of Risk Assessment and Management*, 7 (3). 350–366.

Dalcher, D. (2022) Morality and spirituality. In: Pasian B. and Williams, N. (eds) *Handbook of Responsible Project Management*. Berlin, Germany: De Gruyter.

ECI. (2016) *Global Business Ethics Survey: Measuring Risk and Promoting Workplace Integrity*. Arlington, VA, USA: Ethics & Compliance Initiative.

ECI. (2020) *Global Business Ethics Survey: Pressure in the Workplace: A Global Look*. Arlington, VA, USA: Ethics & Compliance Initiative.

IBE. (2018) *Ethics at Work: 2018 Survey of Employees – Europe*. London, UK: Institute of Business Ethics.

IBE. (2024) *Ethics at Work: 2024 International survey of employees*. London, UK: Institute of Business Ethics.

Martin, M.W. and Schinzinger, R. (2010) *Introduction to Engineering Ethics*. Second edition. New York, NY, USA: McGraw-Hill.

4 ETHICS AND THE IT ORGANISATION

Gillian Arnold and Robert Tripp

This chapter builds on the work of the previous chapter, which considered the ethical behaviour of the IT individual. In this chapter, we consider this person working in an IT organisation. It is split into three parts; first there is a section on the reasons why the IT organisation or department ought to behave ethically. The second part deals with the ethical challenges that a professional in an IT organisation faces and what resources are available to help them. Finally, the third section gives tools and guidance for what the leadership in an IT department needs to put in place.

THE BUSINESS CASE FOR ETHICS WITHIN THE IT DEPARTMENT

As a department, team or organisation, perhaps the IT department couldn't be said to be taking an ethical or unethical decision. Clearly, a 'department' is not able to experience emotions such as love or fear or pain, nor could it be influenced by cognitive reasoning nor social context. However, as explained by Floridi and Sanders (2004), IT departments **are** morally accountable as they can cause effects that can be morally good or bad. The IT department is a collective of individuals and as such is capable of turning out decisions based on the socialisation and moral values of those individuals, influenced by the prevailing culture. Individuals within the department will be required to apply logic, company values and their own personal moral code to make decisions about the software that they manage or build, the services that they provide, the purchases they make and the impact of their actions. Collectively then, the individuals in the IT organisation **do** make moral decisions about their work and its impact, and therefore they can be held responsible for the decisions that are made in the course of their work. However, the decision made collectively, may not be entirely agreeable to, nor the same as that held by the independent members of the department (List and Petit, 2011), and decisions within the team are rarely made by one single individual without reference to various inputs. This dichotomy makes ethical concerns within the IT organisation muddy and unclear. For this reason, individuals within the technical teams need guidance on ethical decision making and the IT leadership needs to ensure that every individual has the support that they need to take sound and ethical decisions. The culture within the department or IT organisation should be such that individuals feel enabled and supported to take the best ethical decisions both for the department and societally.

The implications for reputation and brand

In order to ensure that the whole of the technical team has everything that they require to allow for ethical decision making, the Head of IT will find themselves in discussions with the company's overall senior leadership on the necessity for IT to provide specific support for the IT team around ethical professionalisms (a system sold by Fujitsu to the Post Office). There are disturbing examples of where IT decisions have been made without the underpinning of sound ethical practice. One of the most striking examples of this is the Horizon scandal in the UK which has embroiled both the Post Office and Fujitsu. The Horizon application was known to contain bugs and to be incompletely tested, but somewhere, decisions were taken to ignore this fact within the Post Office, resulting in hugely detrimental impacts to sub-postmasters working with the application. Over 700 sub-postmasters and their families suffered loss of personal financial stability, loss of reputation and in some cases loss of life between 1999 and 2015 and were faced with injustice until the whole scandal came to real public recognition in January 2023. Examples such as this and those in the case studies clearly bring home the far reaching societal impact of IT-based decision making. For both the UK Post Office and Fujitsu it doesn't stop there. For them, as for others taking IT-based decisions with a moral basis, there is the possibility of financial and reputational damage. Fujitsu suffered share price damage and has agreed to work with the UK government on compensation sums for those affected. Senior members of the Post Office leadership team have been castigated publicly and for Paula Vennells, CEO at the time, severe personal loss of reputation. The total compensation required of the Post Office was £58 million but after court costs there is a minimal sum left to compensate the victims of what was an unethical IT decision. At the time of publication the case is still not concluded and might see personal implications for the leaders within the companies. For both organisations, the impacts of the failure to both recognise the issues and then take a sound moral position on software were enormous with regard to brand, revenues and personal liability.

There is also an individual impact at this level. For those involved in ethical decision making or in the build of applications where decisions are impactful society-wide, the comeback on an ethically dubious decision might be loss of personal reputation, or being stripped of professional qualifications and status.

CASE STUDY 4.1: GOOGLE, DECISION MAKING AND A LOSS OF REPUTATION

In 2020, Timnit Gebru, a co-lead for an ethical AI research group at Google, wrote a paper calling out concerns regarding facial recognition software which could identify white men 100 per cent of the time, but which misidentified black women 35 per cent of the time. A dispute ensued and Timnit was fired in December 2020. Whilst there are different interpretations of the course of events from the different players, the decisions which were taken had the result that Google and its decision making on AI bias was covered in the news-media across the world. Timnit Gebru claimed to have been required to resign because of the paper and further staff members resigned due, it was said, to the ethics of the decisions which were taken. There was then an open and external letter with signatures from 2700+ academics and Google employees.

The external notoriety which these ethical decisions around IT caused must have been extremely damaging to Google, who typically would prefer to stay out of the news. In the process it highlighted the extremely poor numbers of people-of-colour employed at Google; way below the national averages, speaking to potential bias in hiring within a large IT organisation.

As Google demonstrates, where ethical decision making is done without reflection on privilege and equality, it can have serious consequences for the brand and reputation of an organisation.

Source: Moss, S. Google AI ethics co-lead says she was fired for raising ethical concerns. Data Center Dynamics. Available from: datacenterdynamics.com/en/news/google-ai-ethics-co-lead-says-she-was-fired-raising-concerns-over-ethics

Financial benefits

The case for ethical IT decision making can also be made around revenues and potential revenues for the company. In the TSB case in Case study 4.2, the damage to brand created significant harm to customer trust and relationships. It became widely public, debated in parliament, scrutinised by a review board, and fines were one of the financial outcomes for the organisation concerned. Where customer trust is damaged by poor IT ethical decision making, it can be difficult, if not impossible to reinstate. The loss of valuable customers has an impact across the business and will have far reaching consequences for years to come.

Employee wellbeing

There is a final aspect to ethical decision making within the IT department. The moral challenge falls to individuals and teams within the organisation. They will want to feel safe within the workplace, safe with the decisions which have been made, and proud of the ethics which are espoused across the division or team. Where this is not true, or where ethical decision making is difficult because it is not supported, employees will feel challenged in their roles, might feel the need to call out the issues they see externally, causing further reputational damage and they might feel a lack of motivation which could lead to attrition of the same staff (see the Tembrit case above).

With all these potential detrimental effects of poor ethical decision making within the IT department it is logical that the leadership within the organisation will want to petition for the resources to support their staff to make informed ethical choices. They will then want to ensure that all aspects of support are in place to facilitate this. The rest of this chapter consists of two sections:

- The next section covers ethical decision making for the IT professionals in their teams.
- The following section provides ethical guidelines, frameworks and processes which will need to be in place specifically for IT decision making.

At the end of the chapter, we provide further reading and sources of material which can be useful to IT leaders and their teams when developing or enhancing ethical practices in the IT team.

CASE STUDY 4.2: TSB BANK

In April 2018, TSB Bank in the UK went live on a new core banking platform for all their 5 million customers in a single migration event. In the days that followed, TSB's Internet Banking and Mobile App channels were 'unstable and almost unusable'. In the second week after go live, TSB had received 33,301 customer complaints, which was 10 times more than usual. In the days and weeks after go live customers experienced opportunistic fraud attacks, which peaked one month after go live, when they were approximately 70 times higher than usual. Slaughter and May were commissioned to carry out an independent report. Some of the findings were:

- The pattern of setting a desired end date and then creating a plan to fit that date, whether or not it was realistic or involved taking too much risk, was set for the remainder of the programme.

- TSB was not transparent about the real reasons behind the decision to delay go live. Having suggested, incorrectly, in September 2017 that the platform would be ready by November 2017, it was made more difficult to announce that the platform was not in fact ready in the lead up to the revised go live date of April 2018.

- During execution of the performance testing for the internet banking and the mobile app, test targets were lowered after tests did not pass at the original target load. The actual volumes following go live exceeded the lowered test targets.

- The TSB Board was not provided with an accurate view of the defects outstanding in the platform at the point of go live; the actual number of defects was at least two and a half times the 'around 800 defects' reported to the TSB Board.

Source: TSB (2019) TSB Board publishes independent review of 2018 IT Migration. Available from tsb.co.uk/news-releases/slaughter-and-may.html.

Somewhere in all this IT professionals lost their moral compass.

THE IT PROFESSIONAL IN THE ORGANISATION

In the previous section we saw examples of how poor or non-existent ethical IT decision making in an organisation can create or destroy value and reputation. The role of IT is not the same in all organisations; in some, such as Google or Amazon Web services or indeed a small software house, the IT is the product the company sells. In these cases the importance of IT ethical decisions is very significant for the organisation and often, as exemplified by Case study 4.4 or with CloudStrike[3], they can have poor societal impacts. The CloudStrike incident was more a sin of omission on the part of the company but in some organisations, the IT is a direct implementation of a poor company-wide ethical policy; the financial services situation mentioned in Case study 4.3 would be an example of this latter category. To be clear, what the organisations were doing in Case study 4.3 was not illegal, but was very far from transparent and the regulator's findings were not that laws were broken, just that customers were not treated fairly. In other organisations IT carries less weight, for example in extractive industries such as mining companies, high street retailers or social care homes, but even in these cases IT still makes important decisions around privacy and security. In 2025 Marks and Spencer, the UK retail group, was the object of a cyberattack that severely impacted their ability to trade and compromised customer data. The attack on the Co-op, another UK retailer, was considerably less damaging because that organisation made better decisions, quicker, a sign that the organisation had spent more time and effort beforehand in scenario planning and taking customer data and service more seriously (Tidy, 2025).

---

3   CloudStrike are a small software company that provides a security component widely used on Microsoft Windows systems. In July 2024 it caused millions of Windows systems in thousands of companies to crash. See techtarget.com/whatis/feature/Explaining-the-largest-IT-outage-in-history-and-whats-next for an explanation.

CASE STUDY 4.3: IT DEVELOPING ETHICALLY BAD REQUIREMENTS – UK MOTOR FINANCE

Writing in 2025, a live issue in the courts and Finance Regulator is the mis-selling of motor finance over the first 20 years of the century. Many people bought cars on leasing deals. These are deals where the consumer gets use of the vehicle but the leasing company owns it and charges them a monthly amount for the period of the lease. In the consumers' eyes this monthly amount was calculated based on the purchase price, the expected value of the car at the end of the lease, the length of the lease and the interest rate. All these factors count but the list is missing a very important item: the commission paid by the finance company to the car dealer or broker to choose them as lender. This was expressed as an additional number of percentages to the interest rate input to the calculation. Even worse, in about 40 per cent of cases the broker could set this commission based on what they thought the customer could/would pay. These commission payments and their amounts were completely invisible to the consumer, even though they could almost double the interest rate.

The monthly payment calculation is complicated and the legal documentation (Consumer Credit Directive) requirements are also complex. The quotation process was all driven by IT shared between the car dealers and the finance companies. IT software developers and project managers built software which took in the commission as a parameter but ensured that no mention of it appeared in any of the consumer-facing documents or screens (e.g. web screens). On the other hand, the commission was all over the dealer and lender screens and reports (e.g. to ensure an accurate split of monies and reconcile bank payments).

On 11 March 2025, the Finance Industry regulator signalled its strong intent to set up a customer redress scheme which is expected to run into billions of pounds in costs to the lenders.

Sources:

Financial Conduct Authority (2025) Statement on motor finance review next steps. Available from: fca.org.uk/news/statements/motor-finance-review-next-steps.

Flanagan, R. (2025) Car finance mis-selling compensation: what you need to know. Which. Available from: which.co.uk/news/article/car-finance-fca-investigation-what-you-need-to-know-a4eXb5u8VeBy.

In either type of organisation the standard excuse for an IT professional collaborating with the organisation on a bad IT project is 'I build what the requirements say; I don't write the requirements'. This is just not good enough; to misquote Thomas Paine, 'The only thing necessary for the triumph of evil is for good men to do nothing'. But more than that, as we see in Chapters 3 and 5, professionals are held to higher standards than day-to-day people. A doctor cannot get away with 'I'm only doing what the hospital management says I must do'. IT professionals cannot behave in this manner and claim to be professional; their professional standards and codes require them to be producing for the common good of society (or at least avoiding harm).

What this means is that IT practitioners working in organisations have to ask themselves questions like 'Will this harm anyone?' or 'Who will be excluded?'. They also have to then deal with negative answers to these questions if they arise. Often it will mean challenging the requirements and the organisational pressures that created those requirements, such as 'Get this code out as quickly as possible' or 'We need to cut the development costs'. Challenging is not easy for a number of reasons as described in the survey results presented in Chapter 3. There are nearly always pressures to cut corners to meet pressing deadlines or reduce costs. There can sometimes be interpersonal problems where the challenge may be perceived by other members of the team or organisation as a criticism of their work or even of their character.

There are lots of other situations where someone in IT is faced with ethical dilemmas, even if they are not completely aware of it. The following are examples:

- **Project managers compromising testing**. As the development phases of projects with a fixed end date slip, it is normal to compromise testing, for example by reducing the planned test cycles or making application and integration testing overlap or run in parallel. It could be argued that this is a business risk decision but as was shown in Case study 4.2 (TSB), sometimes the risks are society wide and IT management have to stand firm for the good of the organisation and society.

- **Not forgetting the digitally excluded**. It is easy to get carried away with a 'mobile first' or digital only strategy because of the low cost to deliver services in a way that is convenient to millions of users 24/7. However there is increasingly an underclass evolving who for a variety of reasons (see Case study 4.5) need to be served as well.

- **Letting end user computing build mission critical applications**. It is common for IT departments to have a finite amount of resources and users with requirements that are a long way down the priority list. A strategy for dealing with this is to allow users to employ end user computing tools to build their own systems and not be subject to the various production readiness checks and testing. This works well with data analytics or process tools which do not have to work 24/7. The risk is that the users start building systems that the organisation becomes critically dependent on and which have not been built to industrial standards (for example, not well documented, do not have high availability in design, do not have a test environment). The IT management have to be unpopular and force such applications to come into the control of the IT standards.

- **A topical issue is 'vibe' programming** (Edwards, 2025), where a user, or indeed a member of the IT department, uses a large language model (LLM) such as ChatGPT to produce code. Some of the risks around this are that nobody knows what has actually been written; has there been an infringement of copyright; is the 'programmer' leaking sensitive information to the wider internet as prompts, ideas and any documentation to specify what is required become ingested by the LLM.

The IT professional can be helped with all these challenges in their ethical dealings with the organisation in two ways:

1. The help from the IT Profession – in the UK, BCS, The Chartered Institute for IT (bcs.org/)

2. The help from the IT leadership team. This is the subject of the next section.

BCS can help. Just being in a profession, citing your professional integrity and that it requires you to challenge the situation is a powerful tool in influencing the organisation. Going back to the medical parallel, suppose a doctor says that they cannot carry out an instruction because it conflicts with their professional code. This is not something that a health service organisation can ignore in the same way as a general employee, such as a clerk or junior manager, can be ignored. The IT professional can point to the BCS Code of Conduct (bcs.org/membership-and-registrations/become-a-member/bcs-code-of-conduct/) that they signed up to. The profession can help in other ways as well:

- BCS can offer training and qualifications that include relevant ethical training and case studies[4].

- BCS offers a network of peers that the IT professional can talk to for independent but relevant advice and support.

---

4   See BCS Foundation Certificate in the Ethical Build of AI. Available at: bcs.org/
    qualifications-and-certifications/online-it-professional-development-courses/
    bcs-foundation-certificate-in-the-ethical-build-of-ai/ (and BCS Foundation
    Award – Understanding ethical principles in the IT profession. Available at:
    bcs.org/qualifications-and-certifications/certifications-for-professionals/
    artificial-intelligence-ai-certifications/artificial-intelligence-foundation-pathway/
    bcs-foundation-award-understanding-ethical-principles-in-the-it-profession/.

- Finally, probably as a last resort, the profession can offer a whistleblowing service if the IT professional feels there is no alternative. This is particularly relevant if a fellow IT professional is the cause of the problem.

As a result of all of the above, the IT profession can empower the IT professional to be better equipped and more confident in dealing with ethical matters whatever the state of the organisation they work in.

Having said that, the IT leadership in the organisation can have a huge influence on whether the IT professional's working environment is one where ethical debates and challenges are welcomed and embraced or not. In the next section we will see some practical suggestions for the IT leadership, but the effects of their actions need to be as follows:

- Individuals in the workforce that feel skilled in tackling relevant ethical issues.

- A widely circulated and understood set of IT organisation ethical principles and values. Some organisations have an organisation-wide code of conduct or set of values. The IT leadership must determine how these can form the basis of principles more specifically relevant to the IT department.

- Evidence that the professionals in the department are supported and encouraged by the leadership in handling these matters. It may be that the organisation takes a different decision to that of the individual but the individual has to feel that their opinion has been heard and the decision has been taken for good reasons. Ethical disagreements are a natural feature of working life; being able to discuss them in a non-threatening environment is vital to building trust.

- The availability of skill development opportunities. Ethical decision making is a skill that improves with practice. The IT organisation needs to find ways to allow their professionals to practise this kind of decision making in a low risk environment so that when faced with real decisions in pressured projects, they are not tackling such problems for the first time.

CASE STUDY 4.4: NEW TECHNOLOGIES AND ETHICAL DESIGN

In her book *The Age of Surveillance Capitalism* (pages 63–85), Shoshana Zuboff explains how in its very early days IT experts at Google used the behavioural data that is a by-product of their users' search activities to improve the service. The data allowed them to create algorithms to predict the users' feelings and intentions when searching, with the aim improving the relevance of search results.

The dot.com crash put pressure on the still tiny Google to find a means to make money quickly. Zuboff explains Google decided to sell advertising slots, using their insights into what users were interested in as an input to deciding which adverts to present. If this were the only factor in deciding which adverts to provide, it would be a logical extension of user service improvement and ethically sound.

However, Google's IT engineers combined these insights with the development of a dynamic, real-time auction to advertisers of the opportunity to advertise in a particular slot. The choice of advert by Google's algorithm would be a function of both the auction price and the user interests with a view to maximising Google's profits. This was ethically much more problematic. The user could not rely on the adverts being presented as being the best for them because an advertiser may just be paying a very high price. Conversely the advertiser has no idea how to compete; they may bid a high price and not get selected.

To be clear, Google's IT wizards were not selling data/ breaking privacy; very far from it. They were monopolising their access to this private data to maximise their profits. A parallel would be a doctor understanding your needs and then recommending the drug that paid the highest commission; a situation that would not be tolerated in the medical profession and should have caused Google's IT professionals food for thought. It set an ethical paradigm for a whole industry.

SUPPORTING ETHICAL DECISION MAKING WITHIN THE IT DEPARTMENT

It will fall to the leadership of the IT team or department to ensure that staff are enabled to make the most appropriate ethical decisions during the course of their work. Leaders will therefore need resources to ensure that they can facilitate this. In this section we suggest ways to take this forward.

The importance of culture

Firstly, the need for sound ethical decision making will be enabled and enhanced by means of the underlying culture of the organisation where it is clear that uncovering unethical practices and making appropriate decisions is a problem which everyone is challenged with and empowered over. Culture can be embedded by means of education and team communications, but there is no more important delineator of culture than the example behaviour of the leadership team. For this reason, when embarking on a new ethical process for the organisation, or when refreshing the old one, the behaviours of the leadership team are crucial to the mix. Forbes (Wallen, 2022) suggests:

> 'With technology advancing at a speed beyond comprehension and human existence operating almost exclusively online, those developing, managing and utilising said technology have a moral responsibility to establish and maintain boundaries to prioritise the human experience over technological gain.'

Some great examples of sound moral decisions and case studies will be useful to share amongst the team. As the department matures in its ethical decision making, these can become home grown examples, but as we show in this chapter, there are several public case studies of ethical IT decision making which can be used until local ones are available. Including these in a reading list which accompanies ethical decision-making training or adding them to team meetings, posters or newsletters are just a few ways of using case studies to exemplify good ethical decision making.

Producing and using a code of ethics

The department will want to make available a code of ethics or principles for professionals to follow. This may be available at a company-wide level, in which case IT should be well represented. However, within the IT department companies will want to ensure that there is an appropriate degree of understanding and effort put into ethics for IT. This starts with a set of core principles that the organisation believes in and is commonly understood. Examples can be found in various places. In his paper *The Code of Data Ethics*, Enrico Panai suggests using beneficence, non-maleficence, autonomy, justice and explicability.

BCS has a different set of four core principles, 'You make IT for everyone; Show what you know, learn what you don't; Respect the organisation or individual you work for; and Keep IT real. Keep IT professional. Pass IT on.'

Both the Panai list and the BCS list of principles mentioned above have longer descriptions of what is to be understood by them. The former can be found in the aforementioned Code of Data Ethics paper by Panai. The latter can be found in the BCS Code of Conduct. There are other sets of core principles from organisations like the Association for Computing Machinery (ACM) and the IEEE Computer Society. The important point is that these principles need to be elaborated and the process of discussing and describing the meaning and implications of the principles is part of creating the organisation's shared set of principles.

Once the principles are agreed, employees could be asked to sign up to these on an annual basis. The belief in, and enforcement of, ethical behaviour in the IT team starts with the leadership team, their example behaviours and the support they put in place. Annual reminders of what is being asked of the team and how the culture is framed by sound ethical behaviour are important. Again, the list of case studies can be included, for example as regular required reading, at this point.

In order to build the internal code of ethics there are several places to find example frameworks. BCS has an ethical code which the team can be asked to sign and this comes with training. The Association of Computer Manufacturers (ACM) also has an extensive code and there is an enormous paper, published by the European Committee for Standardisation (CEN), called the *EU ICT Ethics – European Professional Ethics Framework for the ICT profession*. This paper has hosts of example ethics frameworks which could be used to build one specific to the department or organisation.

When building the code of ethics it is important to have a local team working on the build in order to get buy in. The team might usefully be led by an ethics leader or 'champion' who becomes the figurehead for sound ethical behaviour. In the larger IT departments it would be useful to convene an ethics board which works with the champion to build the best fit for the organisation and which is fully integrated into any company-wide ethics structures.

Checks and balances

The leadership team will want to ensure that ethical checkpoints are included in the IT processes, purchasing, sales and methodologies. They will also want to audit any decision making during the year to ensure that sound morals and ethics were used to undertake the decisions. These of course would need to be free of any degree of self-gain, nepotism or personal conflict of interest. Where staff are raising concerns about decisions made within the department, leaders will want to ensure that there are mechanisms by which staff can remain anonymous where necessary and are protected from situations which would compromise their employment or their safety.

CASE STUDY 4.5: DIGITAL EXCLUSION – THE MORAL DEBATE

The dilemma for IT professionals working on interfaces, gateways and applications for public use is challenging. As the public purse becomes constrained there is more pressure to move applications online and remove the face-to-face opportunities for service users to interact and purchase the services they require. For example, as the UK Driver and Vehicle Licencing Authority (DVLA) closed all of its offices across the country in 2013 and put its services online, it needed to also take a decision to support those users in the UK who did not have access to online services. An example of such a user would be an 84-year-old driver who wanted to obtain vehicle tax but who had no understanding of the technology required to complete the online transaction, nor the computer provision. Equally, a service user who needed to understand the penalty points against their license but could not afford to pay for WIFI or internet facilities, nor the equipment to do so. These cost-to-serve considerations sit with the more senior management, but moral and ethical choices sit with all of us, and the application builders in the IT department have the same professional duty to call out issues which others may not have seen. Certainly, as service builders, all IT professionals must ensure accessibility in the applications and gateways that they build and deliver and should feel enabled to call out the issues that they see. Even if an IT professional may feel they lack influence over a branch closure, they do have power to create a more inclusive range of IT interfaces (for example, including access via Alexa or Siri for the visually impaired).

Building the code of ethics or ethics framework and establishing the work elements

This whole process could usefully be undertaken by means of an ethics 'board' or 'group' which would ideally be made up of a diverse set of individuals in the organisation and of external stakeholders. The example of the Ethics Board at the UK HMRC (His Majesty's Revenue and Customs) is shown in Case study 4.6.

CASE STUDY 4.6: ETHICS AT THE UK REVENUE AND CUSTOMS DEPARTMENT

HMRC is a public body in the UK which deals with the administration and taxation of the populace in all the forms that takes, including direct taxation from wages, VAT, inheritance tax, excise duties etc. It is also a body which investigates fraud and tax evasion and enforces the law around smuggling and money laundering. It is responsible for the collection of nearly £660 billion annually. All staff are expected to work to the HMRC Code of Ethics embedded in the Civil Service Code, and it runs a Professional Standards Committee as a sub-committee of the executive board. The committee is required to consider at least:

- adherence to recognised policy making principles;
- the implementation or operation of government policy, including compliance powers granted by Parliament;
- the implementation or operation of statutory safeguards for taxpayers including rights of review, appeal and redress;
- operational policy and practice;
- the collection and use of data, including data received from third parties, and data-enabled technology;
- the sharing and use of HMRC data beyond HMRC;
- the application of machine learning and artificial intelligence;
- the application of behavioural insight.

Any changes and new initiatives are referred to the Committee.

Source: HMRC Professional Standards Committee – Terms of Reference. Available from: assets.publishing.service.gov.uk/ government/uploads/system/uploads/attachment_data/file/969061/ HMRC_Professional_Standards_Committee_-_Terms_of_Reference.pdf.

The role of the ethics board or committee

When setting up the ethics board or committee it is important to represent various different job roles, seniorities, perspectives and protected characteristics. The HMRC board given in Case study 4.6 reportedly comprises more external stakeholders than internal in 2025. The team might also need access to the legal department or to unions, to product development or customer and supplier representatives. In order to bring this team together, a review of the ethics code of conduct currently in use or a build-from-scratch approach might be taken.

The board/committee should comprise at least a chair or leader who can stand as a figurehead and a secretary or project manager to move tasks forward. In a smaller organisation, the roles and tasks will be more limited and should be tailored accordingly.

Example tasks for the ethics board/committee

- Establish any gaps in the current processes around ethical decision making within the department.

- Decide on the scope of the work being done and who will be impacted.

- Draft and approve the local code of ethics or align with an external one and understand how employees will find it and agree to use it.

- Ensure that there are ethical checkpoints included in the local IT processes and methodologies.

- Anticipate potential areas where ethical dilemmas may occur, looking out for areas of vulnerability or dangers to users of the systems or applications and make these known to staff by means of case studies.

- Publish a list of case studies on ethical IT decision making and replace this eventually with local examples.

- Establish a process which outlines when ethical concerns will be triggered and what to do when they are. The EU ICT Ethics paper *CEN-TS 17834* has a whole example of this.

- Establish a process for auditing ethical decision making on an annual basis.

- Develop a local whistleblowing process, provide escalation points or link to use an external one.

- Elect an ethics champion or leader for the board/committee within the department.

- Ensure that staff are required to agree to the code of ethics annually and make this part of the professional development.

- Commission and undertake ethical training for all and outline who will get which level of education.

- Establish ethical dialogue and communicate the principles to all.

- Build and deploy a communication plan for the department which talks about:

  - Ethical decision making as a responsibility for all.

  - How to integrate ethics in IT into product development and other processes. For example, having some ethical question-based checklists at the key project lifecycle stages such as prior to requirements sign off. Questions in such checklists could include, 'Who might we have accidentally excluded?', 'Would I want to be treated this way by the system?' or 'Would I feel comfortable justifying this to an informed journalist?'.

- How to call out unethical practices.

- What good decision making looks like and sound ethical practices.

- Some case studies.

- Example behaviours from the ethics champion or senior leaders.

• Establish and maintain a register of ethical decisions and issues (see the EU document *CEN-TS 17834* for example register formats).

• Possibly act as an escalation point for ethical dilemmas. This would need support from the executive board, senior stakeholders and legal departments.

Further guidance on the steps which could be taken by the ethics steering board or group can be found in the EU ICT Ethics paper *CEN-TS 17834* in the chapter on Implementing an ICT Ethics Framework in Practice.

Finally, it is important to consider this quote from the Chartered Institute of Professional Development (CIPD, 2015):

'...there is no algorithm for deciding what to do and no option to delegate our dilemmas. ... Thinking about what to do and be is never going to be a mechanical application of a rule: it's always going to require effort, imagination and judgement, and it's often going to be inconclusive'

REFERENCES

BSC Code of Conduct. Available from: bcs.org/membership-and-registrations/become-a-member/bcs-code-of-conduct/.

Clark, S. (2015) Ethical decision-making: Eight perspectives on workplace dilemmas. CIPD. Available from: cipd.org/globalassets/media/comms/the-people-profession/profession-map-pdfs/ethical-decision-making-2015-eight-perspectives-on-workplace-dilemmas_tcm29-9564.pdf.

Edwards, B. (2025) Will the future of software development run on vibes? ars Technica. Available from: arstechnica.com/ai/2025/03/is-vibe-coding-with-ai-gnarly-or-reckless-maybe-some-of-both/.

EU ICT Ethics paper *CEN-TS 17834*. Available from: cencenelec.eu/news-events/news/2022/eninthespotlight/2022-10-10-ict-ethics/.

Financial Conduct Authority. (2025) Statement on motor finance review next steps. Available from: fca.org.uk/news/statements/motor-finance-review-next-steps.

Flanagan, R. (2025) Car finance mis-selling compensation: what you need to know. Which. Available from: which.co.uk/news/article/car-finance-fca-investigation-what-you-need-to-know-a4eXb5u8VeBy.

Floridi, L. and Sanders, L. W. (2004) *Minds and Machines*. New York, NY, USA: Springer International Publishing.

HMRC Professional Standards Committee – Terms of Reference. Available from: assets.publishing.service.gov.uk/government/uploads/system/uploads/attachment_data/file/969061/HMRC_Professional_Standards_Committee_-_Terms_of_Reference.pdf.

Kerner, S. (2024) CrowdStrike outage explained: What caused it and what's next. Available from: techtarget.com/whatis/feature/Explaining-the-largest-IT-outage-in-history-and-whats-next.

List, C. and Petit, P. (2011) *Group Agency*. Oxford, UK: Oxford University Press.

Moss, S. (2020) Google AI ethics co-lead says she was fired for raising ethical concerns. Data Center Dynamics. Available from: datacenterdynamics.com/en/news/google-ai-ethics-co-lead-says-she-was-fired-raising-concerns-over-ethics.

Panai, P. (2023) *The Code of Data Ethics*. New York, NY, USA: ForHumanity.

Tidy, J. (2025) 'They yanked their own plug': How Co-op averted an even worse cyber attack. BBC. Available from: bbc.co.uk/news/articles/cwy382w9eglo.

TSB. (2019) TSB Board publishes independent review of 2018 IT Migration. Available from: tsb.co.uk/news-releases/slaughter-and-may.html.

Wallen, E. (2022) The importance of ethical leadership in tech: A call to action. Forbes. Available from: forbes.com/councils/forbestechcouncil/2022/07/27/the-importance-of-ethical-leadership-in-tech-a-call-to-action/.

5 SOCIETAL RESPONSIBILITIES

Bernd Carsten Stahl

Having established the concepts of ethics within tech, and the individual and corporate perspectives, in this chapter we explore broader societal implications. This chapter is structured in four parts. First, we explore how ethics is rooted in social context, and how professional responsibility extends beyond individual actions. Second, we examine the societal impacts of IT – from economic disruption to political influence and the erosion of human agency. Third, we reflect on the relationship between ethics and law, using human rights as a shared compass while recognising that legal compliance isn't always ethically sufficient. Finally, we consider how we, as professionals, can engage with these challenges – through collective action, inclusive design and public dialogue – to ensure technology serves society as a whole.

While many of the ethical issues and potential harms discussed so far focus on the individual, it is important to keep in mind that ethics is fundamentally a social construct. Individual harms such as those caused by privacy violations, unacceptable discrimination or online bullying and harassment only become recognised if they occur in a social environment where there is agreement that they should be considered to be ethically problematic. Without being able to argue for the social nature of ethics comprehensively and realising that some ethical positions would disagree about the social nature of ethics, we believe that for most practical purposes of an IT professional there is significant social agreement on what counts as harmful and ethically problematic.

The social nature of professional ethics furthermore has strong roots in the idea of professionalism itself. It is the nature of professions that their members are afforded significant advantages, such as a protection of the social status due to their ability to undertake certain tasks. These advantages are normally justified by the fact that they benefit society as a whole. To use the example of a well-established profession, think about a medical doctor. In order to qualify as a medical doctor, one has to undergo significant training and prove technical and other competences. The doctor must undergo rigorous reviews of their work and needs to show they keep up to date and continuously develop their knowledge. This is the basis of the recognition of the doctor as a medical professional, which in most countries is supervised and enforced by rigorous structures that are based on statutory rules. In the UK, for example, a doctor has to register with the General Medical Council to be allowed to practice. In exchange, the medical doctor does not need to worry much about competition. Professions are thus social in nature and require societal recognition and support to function.

These initial remarks are meant to highlight the social nature of the profession and the fact that a professional cannot simply focus exclusively on their area of specialisation and interest. There are different levels of professional organisation across different professions. Computer professionals do not have the same level of duties as well as protection of more established and structured professions such as medicine and law. However, they are still considered professionals. In their role as computer professionals they clearly need to be subject experts and they often have highly detailed expertise in specific areas. However, they need to keep in mind their broader social role and how it relates to their work.

SOCIAL ISSUES OF IT

It is often relatively easy to see where ethical questions arise with regards to specific issues and topics, especially where these relate to a professional's subject expertise. For example, the computer security expert will understand possible vulnerabilities and see how these could lead to violations of data protections and how those, in turn, could lead to harm for users.

It is often much more difficult to see how one's work translates into broader social and societal issues and what the implications of one's technical work are on the broader level. However, as indicated in the introduction to tech ethics chapter, it is important to be aware of the complexity of ethical questions in broader socio-technical ecosystems. It is therefore worth briefly reviewing some of the widely discussed concerns about IT on the societal level.

A good starting point for thinking about societal impact of IT and the ethical questions it raises is the economy. IT has long been a driver of economic development and innovation but in recent years it has become a dominant factor. A strong indicator of the fundamental change of the importance of digital technologies is the capital market. The tech sector, which was virtually non-existent 30 years ago, now dominates today's stock market. Of the top seven companies in the world, all of which had a market capitalisation of more than 1 trillion USD in April 2024, six are tech companies that produce and deploy digital technologies (Microsoft, Apple, NVIDIA, Alphabet, Amazon, Meta) (Companiesmarketcap, 2024). Even allowing for irrational exuberance of markets, this provides a strong indication that digital technology is a key driver of today's economy and, by implication, our society.

While the economic impact of the IT sector is often seen as positive and economic growth is arguably a necessary condition of growing societal welfare, there are significant concerns about possible ethically problematic consequences of ever-widening IT use. One popular topic is the possibility of replacement of humans in economic contexts, leading to unemployment and even more problematically to a kind of ontological redundancy of humanity (Andriole, 2024); see the adjacent box. While the degree to which this is likely to happen is contested (Carroll et al., 2024; Willcocks, 2020), it is without doubt fair to say that it is a key social concern. But while the net employment effects of digital technologies are to some extent an empirical question that we can aim to answer in time, there are further economic concerns. Digital technologies allow structures of work and ownership leading to new business models and use of resources that go beyond what would be possible in a pre-digital economy (Walton and Nayak, 2021). The main point here is that the economic structure changes and these changes can exacerbate pre-existing questions of inequality and justice (AI Council, 2021; Iphofen and Kritikos, 2021). The possibly most prominent critique of these developments was put forward by Zuboff (2019) in her account of what she called surveillance capitalism.

Economic concerns and questions of societal fairness and distribution loom large, but they are by no means the only example of social issues raised by tech. A similarly prominent and often interconnected area is that of politics. The case of Facebook and Cambridge Analytica (Berghel, 2018; Isaak and Hanna, 2018) demonstrated that social media data could be used to illegitimately influence voters and thereby affect election results. Similarly, the generation of fake news through digital technologies has the potential to skew political perceptions and debates (Siau and Wang, 2020). In addition to such technology-enabled interventions into political processes, there are concerns about structural changes to political power and its distribution enabled by digital tech. Much of this is closely interlinked with the concentration of economic power where big tech companies not only dominate the economic sphere but use this influence to exert political power (Coeckelbergh, 2020; Montes and Goertzel, 2019; Nemitz, 2018). The widespread use and analysis of data can furthermore raise concerns about surveillance which can have a 'chilling effect' on human rights and freedoms (Access Now Policy Team, 2018; Muller, 2020).

Ontological redundancy of humanity

This phrase describes what happens when humans are no longer seen as necessary for decision making, care or judgment in technical systems. It's not just about automation replacing jobs – it's about design choices that treat human input as a problem to be engineered away.

As raised in Chapter 2, ethics isn't just about outcomes or rules – it's about what it means to be human in a system. When tools marginalise human discretion or empathy, we risk building processes where no one feels accountable and no one can intervene. This is especially the case in emerging AI systems, where there is a growing perception that generative AI systems can replace human involvement and displace human work.

Ethical IT design preserves space for human agency – not as a fallback, but as a foundation.

Further ethical questions arise in most if not all areas where digital tech is applied. It is important to see that this application of tech is normally driven by an expectation that it will lead to an improvement of performance but that this improvement is accompanied by an assumption that it will have beneficial effects. A key challenge arising from this assumption that it is often impossible to assess what exactly the consequences of the use of a technology are, even if it is already established and widely diffused. In order to fully understand those, it would be necessary to be able to compare a given social group using control groups that use and don't use the technology. This sort of situation that would allow an empirical investigation of detailed consequences is rarely if ever available. One of the most difficult social consequences to assess from an ethical and professional perspective is the way in which digital technology shapes our perceptions of ourselves and how it shapes our ability to act. Technology can acquire power over humans by allowing some activities while limiting others

(Waelen, 2022, p. 7). The tech we use not only influences what we do and can do, but also how we see ourselves and what we perceive to be the space of possibilities and options available to us (Coeckelbergh, 2019). Some digital interventions explicitly aim to do this, for example by offering new ways to connect and communicate. They may also close off options, but these are often less visible and difficult to ascertain.

The point to keep in mind here is that not only are there social consequences arising from tech, but the exact nature of these consequences can be difficult to ascertain and may only become clear retrospectively, many years in the future. This makes it very difficult for IT professionals to proactively engage with these questions. Before we return to ways of doing this, it is important to touch on one critical factor that influences how social issues in IT are perceived and dealt with, namely the law.

ETHICS AND THE LAW IN IT

This book is about tech ethics and not about tech law, on which there are numerous other publications. However, many of the issues that are perceived to be ethically relevant have a legal angle to them. We said earlier that ethical issues are often those that are related to possible harms. Where harms become prevalent, societies tend to intervene using legal measures to prevent or mitigate the harm.

The relationship of ethics and the law is subject to specialised discourses which we cannot recount here. For the perspective of this book it will suffice to see ethics, professionalism and legislation as separate but often overlapping ways that societies use to deal with problems and challenges. Legislation passed by a national legislature has the highest level of formality and is normally endowed with enforcement mechanisms, including legal sanctions for infringements. Not everything can always be legislated which is one of the reasons why societies make use of other mechanisms, including professionalism. In many cases the basis of professionalism, or aspects of it, is the law.

For example, professional bodies that have strong means of enforcement of professional rules tend to have a legal basis.

In cases of legitimate and democratic legal systems, the starting assumption is that the law is just and appropriate. It is therefore the duty of all citizens including professionals to adhere to the law. The commitment to the public good that underpins professionalism puts an added onus on professionals to comply with the law and sanctions for breaking it tend to be higher for professionals, who can lose their professional status for legal infractions.

There are different types of law, such as criminal law, civil law or administrative law which have different levels of relevance to the type of questions that tech ethics deals with. One particular body of law of high relevance and visibility is that of human rights law. Human rights, which were first codified in the wake of the Second World War (United Nations, 1948), are arguably expressions of underlying ethical convictions and represent a world-wide consensus on what counts as morally right. Such a moral consensus can be invaluable for professionals when trying to work out which issues to consider and how to deal with them during the development and deployment of digital technology. This may explain why there is significant emphasis on human rights in the current discussion of dealing with the ethical issues of AI (Access Now Policy Team, 2018; OECD, 2019). Human rights have the added advantage that they are typically reflected in national law and provide access to enforcement mechanisms.

It is thus fair to say that tech professionals should consider the impact of their work on human rights. This covers many of the well-established possible harms arising from tech, such as invasions of privacy or unfair discrimination. A key challenge will often be the translation of the typically rather abstract description of human rights into practices of tech development and use. However, these practical challenges do not affect the role of human rights as a normative anchor point. In addition, and in line with most ethical guidance, professionals should comply with the legislation that governs the jurisdiction that they operate in.

Having said this, we want to raise a caveat. The assumption that the law is just and we have a moral duty to obey it is no doubt a useful starting point. However, professionals may encounter situations where this starting point is doubtful. This may be the case where professionals work across jurisdiction and laws compete or contradict each other or where the origin of the law lacks legitimacy, which is typically the case in authoritarian and dictatorial regimes.

To complicate matters further, we need to concede that even laws in democratic countries are the outcomes of political conflict and can be unjust or morally problematic. The use of surveillance technologies targeted at foreigners or automated decision support for offender management may constitute such problematic examples. These may be mandated or allowed by legitimate democratic process of legislation and regulation, but they may be ethically objectionable. In such cases a professional may feel that they have a moral duty to challenge the basis for the use of the technology in such a way or – in extreme cases – they may perceive a duty to disobey the law. Such dilemma situations can arise and professional guidance may help the professional to navigate them, but they rarely have clear-cut options and solutions.

When faced with laws or organisational policies that seem unjust, such as those enabling algorithmic discrimination or restricting digital access, professionals must draw on ethical frameworks to guide principled dissent. Reflecting back to Chapter 2, a deontological perspective could insist that upholding human dignity and fundamental rights takes precedence over mere compliance. A virtue ethicist may ask, 'What would a just and courageous professional do in this situation?' Meanwhile, a consequentialist might weigh the potential harm of remaining silent against the risks of speaking out. Whichever lens is used, difficult choices must often be made. That's why Chapter 4's discussion of professional support systems, such as ethics boards, peer communities or whistleblowing mechanisms, is so vital. When legal compliance conflicts with ethical responsibility, these structures can contribute to both moral clarity and institutional backing.

As technologists shaping the infrastructures of society, our obligations cannot end where legal obligations begin.

Translating human rights into software design isn't always straightforward but many everyday IT practices directly implicate specific rights enshrined in international frameworks like the Universal Declaration of Human Rights (UDHR) or the European Convention on Human Rights (ECHR). For instance, algorithmic profiling used in recruitment or lending decisions touches on the right to non-discrimination (Article 14 ECHR) and the right to fair treatment (Article 6 ECHR). If opaque algorithms reinforce historic bias, the result can be widespread exclusion without clear recourse. Similarly, data retention policies implicate the right to privacy (Article 8 ECHR / Article 12 UDHR), especially when data is kept far longer than necessary or repurposed without consent. Meanwhile, platform governance decisions, like moderating harmful content or banning users, engage the right to freedom of expression (Article 10 ECHR / Article 19 UDHR), which must be balanced against safety, dignity and protection from harm. IT professionals don't need to be lawyers, but a working understanding of how their design choices affect rights – and who is most likely to be impacted– can turn abstract ideals into daily due diligence. Ethical IT design is human rights in practice.

POSSIBLE WAYS OF ADDRESSING SOCIAL RESPONSIBILITIES

The purpose of this chapter was to move the focus of attention away from the individual and technical issues that often dominate the discussion and explore the social nature of professionalism and the challenges that professionals may face. This raises the question of what a professional can do to understand such social questions, maybe predict or pre-empt them and find appropriate ways of dealing with them.

The social nature of these broader issues and resulting responsibilities means that it cannot be down to the individual to comprehensively address them. In many cases they call for organisational, industry-wide or societal responses that typically have a strong political component. Questions of distribution of resources, political power, environmental impacts, changing patterns of work, and so on, call for national and international policy and regulation.

However, this does not mean that the individual professional has no role to play. It is part of the professional ethos and its commitment to the public good to take a prominent role in such discourses. Such professional engagement can take many forms, for example the contribution to standard setting, activity in professional bodies which, in turn, tend to contribute to policy discourses, or using one's professional experience to support the quality and veracity of political discussions. In order to be able to do this, the professional not only needs their subject knowledge to be current, but also to understand the social context of their work, including the legal environment and the socio-technical ecosystem in which they move. Addressing social issues arising from digital technologies will typically involve dealing with dilemmas and contradictions between opposing legitimate interests. Responses will thus rarely be straightforward. In order to gain legitimacy, they will need to involve those who are affected, thus calling for stakeholder involvement which will typically include the processes of representative democracy, but may also go beyond those and draw on the rich field of public engagement methods. The onus is not on the individual professional to realise such broader engagement but as a professional they can be legitimately expected to be part of them and contribute to them.

To move beyond individual reflection and into collective accountability, IT professionals and their organisations can adopt structured frameworks for assessing societal impact and engaging with diverse stakeholders. Tools such as socio-technical impact assessments – used in public sector projects and research ethics boards – encourage multidisciplinary review of how systems might reinforce inequality, limit autonomy or shift public norms. Frameworks like STIR (Socio-Technical Integration Research) (Fisher et al., 2006) embed ethical enquiry directly into development teams, fostering dialogue between technologists and social scientists. For broader stakeholder engagement, models such as Value Sensitive Design (VSD) (Friedman et al., 2008; Gerdes and Frandsen, 2023) or the Responsible Innovation framework (which includes anticipation, inclusion, reflexivity and responsiveness) (Jirotka et al., 2017; Stilgoe et al., 2013) offer practical steps to surface competing interests and unintended harms early. Professionals can also support or convene citizen juries, design charrettes or ethics sandboxes – spaces where public voices shape technology trajectories. These practices help ensure that 'engagement' is not just consultation after the fact, but a meaningful influence on what gets built, for whom and why.

While much of this chapter has focused on recognising and responding to ethical risks, being a responsible IT professional is about using IT positively, whilst avoiding harm. Technology, when developed with care, creativity and a commitment to justice, can be a profound force for societal benefit. Whether through building accessible platforms, designing systems that support underserved communities or using AI to accelerate climate solutions, professionals have the capacity – and responsibility – to contribute positively to the world we share. The next chapter explores how this proactive vision can be embedded into the everyday practice of sustainable, ethical technology design that considers the wider impact of technology on the world, and how this can be used to proactively address some of today's global challenges.

REFERENCES

Access Now. (2018) *Human Rights in the Age of Artificial Intelligence*. Available from: accessnow.org/wp-content/uploads/2018/11/AI-and-Human-Rights.pdf.

Access Now Policy Team. (2018) *The Toronto Declaration: Protecting the Right to Equality and Non-Discrimination in Machine Learning Systems*. Toronto, Canada: Access Now.

AI Council. (2021) *AI Roadmap*. London, UK: Office for Artificial Intelligence, Department for Business, Energy and Industrial Strategy, and Department for Digital, Culture, Media and Sport.

Andriole, S.J. (2024) 'The big miss: AI will replace just about everything'. *Communications of the Association for Information Systems*, 55 (1). 29.

Berghel, H. (2018) 'Malice domestic: The Cambridge analytica dystopia'. *Computer*. The IEEE Computer Society, 51 (05). 84–89.

Carroll, N., Holmström, J., Stahl, B. and Fabian, N. (2024) 'Navigating the utopia and dystopia perspectives of artificial intelligence'. *Communications of the Association for Information Systems*, 55 (1). 854–874.

Coeckelbergh, M. (2019) Technology, narrative and performance in the social theatre. In: Kreps, D. (ed.) *Understanding Digital Events: Bergson, Whitehead, and the Experience of the Digital*. First edition. New York, NY, USA: Routledge. 13–27.

Coeckelbergh, M. (2020) *AI Ethics*. Cambridge, MA, USA: The MIT Press.

Companiesmarketcap. (2024) Companies ranked by Market Cap. Available from: companiesmarketcap.com/.

Fisher, E., Mahajan, R.L. and Mitcham, C. (2006) 'Midstream modulation of technology: Governance from within'. *Bulletin of Science, Technology & Society*, 26 (6). 485–496, doi: 10.1177/0270467606295402.

Friedman, B., Kahn, P. and Borning, A. (2008) Value sensitive design and information systems. In: Himma, K. and Tavani, H. (eds) *The Handbook of Information and Computer Ethics*. Hoboken, NJ, USA: Wiley Blackwell. 69–102.

Gerdes, A. and Frandsen, T.F. (2023) 'A systematic review of almost three decades of value sensitive design (VSD): What happened to the technical investigations?'. *Ethics and Information Technology*, 25 (2). 26. doi: 10.1007/s10676-023-09700-2.

Iphofen, R. and Kritikos, M. (2021) 'Regulating artificial intelligence and robotics: Ethics by design in a digital society'. *Contemporary Social Science*, 16 (2). 170–184, doi: 10.1080/21582041.2018.1563803.

Isaak, J. and Hanna, M.J. (2018) 'User data privacy: Facebook, Cambridge Analytica, and privacy protection'. *Computer*, 51 (8). 56–59.

Jirotka, M., Grimpe, B., Stahl, B., Hartswood, M. and Eden, G. (2017) 'Responsible research and innovation in the digital age'. *Communications of the ACM*. 60 (5). 62–68, doi: 10.1145/3064940.

Montes, G.A. and Goertzel, B. (2019) 'Distributed, decentralized, and democratized artificial intelligence'. *Technological Forecasting and Social Change*, 141. 354–358, doi: 10.1016/j. techfore.2018.11.010.

Muller, C. (2020) *The Impact of Artificial Intelligence on Human Rights, Democracy and the Rule of Law*. Strasbourg, France: No. CAHAI(2020)06-fin, Council of Europe, Ad Hoc Committee on Artificial Intelligence (CAHAI).

Nemitz, P. (2018) 'Constitutional democracy and technology in the age of artificial intelligence'. *Philosophical Transactions of the Royal Society A*, 376 (2133). 20180089, doi: 10.1098/rsta.2018.0089.

OECD. (2019) *Recommendation of the Council on Artificial Intelligence*. OECD Legal Instruments, OECD.

Siau, K. and Wang, W. (2020) 'Artificial intelligence (AI) ethics: Ethics of AI and ethical AI'. *Journal of Database Management (JDM)*, IGI Global, 31 (2). 74–87.

Stilgoe, J., Owen, R. and Macnaghten, P. (2013) 'Developing a framework for responsible innovation'. *Research Policy*, 42 (9). 1568–1580. doi: 10.1016/j.respol.2013.05.008.

United Nations. (1948) *Universal Declaration of Human Rights*.

Waelen, R. (2022) 'Why AI ethics is a critical theory'. *Philosophy & Technology*, 35 (1). 9. doi: 10.1007/s13347-022-00507-5.

Walton, N. and Nayak, B.S. (2021) 'Rethinking of Marxist perspectives on big data, artificial intelligence (AI) and capitalist economic development'. *Technological Forecasting and Social Change*, 166. 120576. doi: 10.1016/j.techfore.2021.120576.

Willcocks, L. (2020) 'Robo-apocalypse cancelled? Reframing the automation and future of work debate'. *Journal of Information Technology*, SAGE Publications Ltd, 35 (4). 286–302. doi: 10.1177/0268396220925830.

Zuboff, S. (2019) *The Age of Surveillance Capitalism: The Fight for a Human Future at the New Frontier of Power*. First edition. London, UK: Profile Books.

6 SUSTAINABLE AND ETHICAL PRACTICES IN TECHNOLOGY

Neil Gordon

Following on from the previous chapter where social responsibilities and issues were explored, in this chapter we consider broader global issues. Firstly, we introduce the ethical significance of sustainability in computing, framing it within global perspectives. Secondly, we distinguish between green IT and sustainable IT, and why both matter. Thirdly, we explore the broader concept of sustainable development and its relevance to technology ethics and IT professionals. With real-world case studies we illustrate the positive and negative impacts of ethical and sustainable practices in technology. Finally, we map computing's potential contributions to each of the 17 Sustainable Development Goals (SDGs) and outline practical actions for companies, governments and policy makers, professionals and individuals to move toward more ethical and sustainable tech practices.

INTRODUCTION: WHY SUSTAINABILITY MATTERS IN IT

Does what we do as individuals matter? In this chapter we consider some of the ethical challenges faced in the IT industry. Computing is a global industry with a significant impact on human society and the natural environment. These global impacts can seem out of our control, but as individuals we have responsibilities and the potential to have an impact.

This chapter considers these challenges in the context of global computing, and how initiatives such as the United Nations (UN) Sustainable Development activities can provide a context within which to direct our actions. This global viewpoint reflects BCS's motto of 'making IT good for society', but from a wider perspective. In this chapter we define sustainability in technology and how this goes beyond just energy efficiency. We will explore why ethical responsibility includes sustainability and this intersection of ethics, sustainability and corporate/social responsibility.

Technology is an integral part of modern life, shaping industries, economies and everyday interactions. However, this rapid digital transformation comes at a cost – environmentally, socially and ethically. Sustainable IT refers to the responsible design, development and use of technology that minimises its negative impact on the planet while promoting long-term social and economic wellbeing. Beyond just reducing carbon footprints, technology plays a fundamental role in achieving global sustainability goals, particularly the UN SDGs (UN, 2022) – a blueprint for addressing poverty, inequality, climate change and sustainable economic growth. This chapter explores what sustainable IT entails, why it is a moral imperative and how technology can both help and harm the world.

GREEN AND SUSTAINABLE IT: WHAT THEY ARE AND HOW THEY DIFFER

Green IT

You may be familiar with green computing or green IT, which focusses on the environmental impact of computing. This is an important aspect, and the carbon footprint and wider environmental impact of computing is something we should all consider when developing solutions and recommending systems (Murugesan and Gangadharan, 2012).

Green IT refers to the design, use and disposal of technology in an environmentally responsible way. It aims to minimise the ecological impact of computing by focusing on energy efficiency, e-waste reduction, ethical sourcing and sustainable software development. When using systems, we should have these in mind and consider different approaches to minimise the potential damage that computing causes. Some of the key aspects of green IT include:

- **Energy-efficient computing** – Optimising hardware and software to reduce power consumption. Developing low-energy hardware, optimising software and using cloud computing solutions where that is optimal. Technologies from search engines to AI, and cryptocurrencies to multimedia streaming are all using increasing data processing, data transmission and associated processing overheads (Belkhir and Elmeligi, 2018).
- **Green and sustainable data centres** – Companies investing in renewable energy-powered infrastructure and efficient cooling technologies. Using renewable energy and AI-driven cooling systems to cut carbon emissions (ITU and World Bank, 2023).
- **E-waste management** – Encouraging recycling, refurbishment and the right to repair.
- **Eco-friendly supply chains** – Ensuring ethical sourcing of raw materials and fair labour conditions.
- **Sustainable software practices** – Writing efficient code to reduce processing power demands, thereby reducing the need to upgrade and lowering energy consumption (Podder and Balani, 2024).

By considering the entire lifecycle of technology, from material sourcing to disposal, sustainable IT aims to create a more responsible digital ecosystem (Software Improvement Group, 2024).

Sustainable IT

Sustainable IT is sometimes considered as synonymous with green IT but should be thought of as a broader concept, though it can be considered to encompass it. Sustainable IT is a larger concept that includes environmental, social and economic sustainability. It aligns with long-term digital responsibility and the UN SDGs (Gordon, 2010; Sachs, 2015).

In addition to green IT, sustainable IT considers aspects such as:

- **Digital inclusion** – Ensuring fair access to technology and bridging the digital divide.

- **Sustainable business models** – Ethical sourcing, fair wages and corporate social responsibility.

- **Circular economy in tech** – Designing products for reuse, repair and recycling.

- **Responsible AI and automation** – Ensuring that AI-driven solutions support sustainability rather than exacerbate inequalities (Floridi et al., 2018).

- **Ethical software development** – Avoiding dark patterns, reducing unnecessary computing requirements that could require non-essential upgrades and ensuring privacy/security (Gogoll et al., 2021).

So sustainable IT can be summarised as technology that supports environmental, social and economic sustainability (Mobbs, 2012; Software AG, 2023).

Key differences

Table 6.1 The key differences between green and sustainable IT

Aspect	Green IT	Sustainable IT
Focus area	Environmental impact (carbon emissions, energy use, e-waste)	Holistic sustainability (environment, economy, society)
Main goal	Reduce technology's ecological footprint	Ensure long-term responsible digital transformation
Key practices	Energy-efficient computing, recycling, eco-friendly manufacturing	Ethical labour, digital inclusion, sustainable AI, green IT
Scope	Narrower (mostly environmental)	Broader (includes ethical and social factors)

Why both matter

Green IT helps reduce carbon footprints and waste, whilst sustainable IT ensures technology is fair, ethical and accessible for all.

SUSTAINABLE DEVELOPMENT AND THE SUSTAINABLE DEVELOPMENT GOALS

Given the global focus of this chapter, and the sustainable computing aspect, we now consider briefly what this is and how individuals can contribute.

What is sustainable development?

Sustainable development is a way of meeting present needs 'without compromising the ability of future generations' to meet their own needs. It balances 'economic growth, social wellbeing and environmental protection' to create a long-term, liveable future. This has been couched in terms of three pillars:

1. **Environmental sustainability** – Protecting natural resources, reducing pollution and addressing climate change.

2. **Social sustainability** – Ensuring fair access to education, healthcare and basic human rights.

3. **Economic sustainability** – Promoting responsible economic growth, fair labour practices and innovation.

Whilst the world's nations signed up to the original sustainable development concept, this lacked specific targets. However, these were later developed through the SDGs. The UN's 17 SDGs provide a global framework to address poverty, inequality, climate change and sustainability.

Why is sustainable development relevant to tech ethics?

Sustainable development has the potential to ensure a healthy planet, thriving societies and resilient economies for future generations. It requires collaboration between governments, businesses and individuals to create long-term solutions. We will consider how computing can play a role in all 17 goals to attempt to achieve this, and you can consider what role you could play. The ethos that underpins sustainable development and led to the SDGs can provide a framework for helping to direct our own actions and choices (Gordon, 2014).

Technology's environmental and ethical footprint extends beyond carbon emissions. The rapid consumption and disposal of digital devices raise serious ethical concerns:

- **E-waste crisis** – The world generates over 50 million metric tons of e-waste annually, much of it exported to developing countries, leading to toxic pollution and hazardous working conditions.

- **Unethical supply chains** – Many electronic devices rely on minerals such as cobalt and lithium, often mined under exploitative conditions, including child labour and unsafe working environments.

- **Digital divide and economic disparity** – Many developing nations lack access to affordable and sustainable computing resources, widening economic and social inequalities (Selwyn, 2004).

By prioritising sustainable IT, companies and individuals can align their practices with ethical responsibility, human rights and global sustainability goals.

HOW CAN WE ACT IN A SUSTAINABLE WAY AS IT PROFESSIONALS?

The UN's Sustainable Development initiative outlines several issues and challenges that reflect a global view of equity, fairness and need. As practitioners, we can consider how our own work fits into that, and whether we are enabling and supporting these, or even potentially acting against them.

As a global industry, national interests and perspectives provide the context for individuals, but we should still consider the bigger picture and the potential impact of our work beyond our immediate context. For example, the climate impact affects other countries and people – often the most vulnerable are the least able to adapt to this.

There are numerous examples of technologies that have global impacts, from social media to the release of generative AI models. If quantum computing fulfils its promise soon, the impact of that on the digital world and global financial systems will cross national borders.

Whilst the tech industry is huge with many companies and individuals, there are a number of dominant companies responsible for operating systems, key aspects of hardware and software, and thereby having an impact across borders. We also have to consider issues of resilience and national security – where cloud platforms and AI systems are accessed from other countries and thus potentially undermine national independence and resilience.

In determining IT solutions there are choices between Open Software versus commercial and proprietary software. The need to be professional and identify the best solution can raise issues around the meaning of best – where simple financial cost may not capture the wider perspective of better. Similarly, choices of whether to use a cloud solution or a local device are hard to make where there isn't clear data to compare the overall environmental cost of building, running and using the different systems.

Ethical choices can be clear when things have obvious ethical implications, such as misuse of users' data. Others may only become apparent as the impacts are recognised. The systems may be ones that have obvious ethical challenges – such as computer controlled weapons, to those that seem more mundane but can have terrible consequences.

Some recent examples of negative impacts from IT systems include:

1. The bugs that lay behind the failures in the UK's Post Office Horizon system (Williams, 2025). Here failures in that system led to users (Post Office sub-postmasters) being wrongly accused of theft. The legal court cases built on this led to imprisonment and terrible impacts on the lives of the accused and their families, and is attributed as the cause of five to 13 suicides to date (iNews, 2025). This example illustrates the issues of IT providers and the companies they supply failing to recognise and acknowledge limitations and potential issues in their systems, and that those involved could have raised this prior to the legal action on people based on this erroneous data.

2. The algorithms that make social media so popular and effective have been identified as leading to genocide, in the case of Rohingya and FaceBook (Amnesty International, 2022). This example shows unintended consequences in the context of differing world views on issues such as corporate responsibility and the impact of technology.

3. The diesel emissions scandal where engine management software was written to adapt engine performance to evade stringent emissions tests (Oppenhoff, 2023). This example illustrates a corporation deliberately implementing hardware and software to attempt to evade legislative systems.

4. The Boeing737 Max where a mix of faulty software combined with faulty sensors has been identified as the cause of plane crashes and tragic loss of life (Larcker and Tayan, 2024). The solution was a software fix illustrating the terrible consequences of software in modern systems.

These examples have focussed on the negative. This is to help emphasise the importance of professionals and companies taking account of the impact of their work. Technology can be a force for good, as we consider in the following case studies.

CASE STUDIES: THE GOOD AND BAD OF TECHNOLOGY

These case studies highlight the impact of sustainable and ethical practices in technology. Some are positive, others negative – though individual perspectives on right and wrong will differ at times.

CASE STUDY 6.1: GOOGLE'S CARBON-NEUTRAL DATA CENTRES (THE GOOD)

The challenge

Data centres consume enormous amounts of electricity, contributing significantly to carbon emissions. These are essential to cloud computing, shared databases and web-based services such as many of the AI models.

The solution

Google has committed to operating all of its data centres with 100 per cent carbon-free energy by 2030. The company has implemented AI-powered cooling systems, optimised hardware for efficiency and invested in renewable energy sources such as wind and solar.

The impact

This has seen a reduction in data centre energy consumption by 40 per cent (*Wired*, 2016). Google became the largest corporate purchaser of renewable energy worldwide. This has demonstrated that AI can improve energy efficiency in large-scale IT operations.

Lesson learned

Large tech firms can leverage AI and sustainable infrastructure to minimise their environmental impact, setting an industry standard. As a note to this, whilst AI enabled that saving, the increased use of Google's AI service is now attributed to a 51 per cent rise in its emissions (*The Guardian*, 2025) illustrating the complexities of competing and sometimes incompatible activities.

CASE STUDY 6.2: THE E-WASTE CRISIS IN AGBOGBLOSHIE, GHANA (THE BAD)

The challenge

Agbogbloshie, Ghana, is one of the world's largest e-waste dumping sites. Much of this electronic waste comes from developed countries that export discarded electronics to Africa under the pretence of 'reuse' (Balde et al., 2017).

The consequences

Workers – often children – burn toxic materials to extract valuable metals, exposing themselves to hazardous chemicals.

The impact

This has led to air, soil and water pollution from lead, mercury and other toxins. A consequence of this is high rates of respiratory diseases, neurological damage and cancer among workers. Alongside the health issues are violations of human rights and environmental justice principles.

Lesson learned

Developed countries must take responsibility for their e-waste exports, enforce strict regulations and support ethical recycling programmes instead of dumping waste in the Global South.

CASE STUDY 6.3: FAIRPHONE – ETHICAL ELECTRONICS (THE GOOD)

The challenge

Many smartphone manufacturers use minerals sourced from mines with exploitative labour conditions and design devices for obsolescence, making repairs difficult. Fairphone is a company that designs modular, repairable smartphones with ethically sourced materials.

The solution

Fairphone produces modular smartphones that:

- use ethically sourced materials, including Fairtrade gold and conflict-free tungsten;

- allow users to replace batteries, screens and cameras without professional repairs;

- ensure fair wages and ethical supply chain transparency.

The impact

This has led to smartphone devices with extended lifespans, reducing e-waste. It has also pushed the industry toward more sustainable production (influencing companies like Apple to introduce repair kits) (Proske et al., 2020). Overall this has demonstrated a viable business model for sustainable electronics.

Lesson learned

Consumer demand for ethical and sustainable tech can drive industry-wide change toward more responsible production practices.

CASE STUDY 6.4: CRYPTOCURRENCY'S ENVIRONMENTAL TOLL (THE BAD)

The challenge

While blockchain technology has many positive applications, Bitcoin mining consumes more electricity than some entire countries. The proof-of-work system requires massive computational power, contributing significantly to carbon emissions. Critics argue that unless cryptocurrency moves toward more energy-efficient models, its environmental impact will continue to rise.

The consequences

Bitcoin mining consumes more electricity than some entire countries, like Argentina or the Netherlands. Much of this is powered by fossil-fuel-based electricity, increasing carbon footprints and contributing to climate change. Crypto farms often drain local energy resources, leading to higher electricity costs for residents.

Lesson learned

Some cryptocurrencies (such as Ethereum) have transitioned to proof-of-stake, a model that was claimed to reduce energy consumption by over 99 per cent, though this figure is not certain (Forbes, 2023). Governments are regulating energy-intensive crypto operations, encouraging greener alternatives. Emerging technologies must consider sustainability from the start to prevent unintended environmental consequences.

CASE STUDY 6.5: SMART CITIES AND SUSTAINABLE URBAN TECH (THE GOOD)

The challenge

As urban populations grow, cities face traffic congestion, pollution and inefficient resource management.

The solution

Cities like Singapore and Copenhagen have integrated AI, Internet of Things (IoT) and data analytics to create sustainable urban environments (Vanli, 2024).

- Smart traffic systems reduce congestion and emissions.
- IoT-enabled waste management ensures efficient garbage collection.
- Renewable energy microgrids make cities more energy-efficient.

The impact

Reduced carbon footprints by 30 per cent in some regions. Improved public transportation efficiency. Enhanced quality of life through green urban planning.

Lesson learned

Technology can be a force for good when designed with sustainability in mind, improving both environmental and social wellbeing.

SUSTAINABLE COMPUTING

The case studies highlight both the positive and negative impacts of technology. These illustrate issues where tech can be the cause of problems, and others where it can be a solution. They show the need to:

- encourage corporate sustainability commitments (like Google and Fairphone);
- advocate for ethical labour practices in tech supply chains;
- support green innovations like AI-driven energy efficiency;
- reduce reliance on environmentally harmful technologies, such as energy-intensive cryptocurrencies;
- push for stronger global policies on e-waste and ethical manufacturing and for reliable and trustworthy data to validate claimed improvements.

Following from this, we now map all the current SDGs to various areas where computing that can have a positive impact.

Computing technologies can play an essential role in advancing all 17 SDGs. From AI, data analytics and IoT to blockchain and cloud computing, these technologies help drive sustainability, equity and innovation across all sectors of society and across the planet. As digital technologies continue to evolve, their ability to support global sustainable development will only grow, making them crucial tools in shaping a more sustainable, equitable and prosperous future for all.

Table 6.2 Examples of computing's potential impact on areas of the Sustainable Development Goals

#SDG	Description	Examples of computing's potential impact
1	No poverty	• Mobile banking and fintech can provide financial services to unbanked populations. • E-learning platforms can provide access to education for marginalised communities, opening up job opportunities. • Digital platforms for microloans can support small-scale entrepreneurs in impoverished regions.
2	Zero hunger	• AI and data analytics optimise agriculture production, reducing waste and improving crop yields. • Precision farming technologies (e.g. IoT sensors) reduce the environmental footprint of agriculture. • Supply chain management software reduces food waste by ensuring better distribution of resources.
3	Good health and wellbeing	• Telemedicine and e-health systems enhance access to healthcare, especially in rural or remote areas. • AI-based diagnostics can improve early detection of diseases, such as cancer and heart conditions. • Data analytics and big data can track and predict health trends, improving public health strategies.

(Continued)

Table 6.2 (Continued)

#SDG	Description	Examples of computing's potential impact
4	Quality education	• E-learning platforms and online courses make education accessible to all, especially in underdeveloped areas. • AI and personalised learning systems can adapt educational content to suit individual learning needs. • Digital textbooks and open-source educational resources can lower the cost of education globally.
5	Gender equality	• Digital platforms can empower women with financial independence, education and entrepreneurship opportunities. • AI-powered tools can highlight gender inequality and support the development of gender-sensitive policies. • Online communities and social media help amplify women's voices, advocate for gender equality and combat online harassment.
6	Clean water and sanitation	• IoT sensors can monitor water quality and help manage water distribution systems more efficiently. • Data analytics helps track water usage and detect leaks or inefficiencies in water systems. • Mobile apps can improve access to sanitation facilities and raise awareness of water conservation.

(Continued)

Table 6.2 (Continued)

#SDG	Description	Examples of computing's potential impact
7	Affordable and clean energy	• Smart grids use AI and IoT to improve energy distribution and incorporate renewable energy sources. • Big data can forecast energy demand, optimising the use of clean energy. • Energy-efficient computing technologies (e.g. cloud computing) can reduce the IT sector's carbon footprint.
8	Decent work and economic growth	• Digital platforms provide access to jobs and promote remote working and the gig economy. • AI and automation drive productivity improvements in various sectors, enhancing economic growth. • Fintech solutions like cryptocurrency and blockchain provide financial inclusion for underserved regions.
9	Industry, innovation and infrastructure	• Green IT reduces energy consumption in digital infrastructure. • Digital transformation of industries enables sustainable manufacturing, with AI, robotics and IoT reducing waste and improving resource efficiency. • Smart city technologies (e.g. IoT, 5G networks) improve urban infrastructure, making cities more resilient and sustainable.

(Continued)

Table 6.2 (Continued)

#SDG	Description	Examples of computing's potential impact
		• Cloud computing enables innovation by making computing power and data storage more accessible to small businesses.
10	Reduced inequality	• Digital technologies can connect marginalised communities to education, healthcare and economic opportunities, reducing social inequality.
		• AI and data analytics can help identify inequalities in access to resources and services.
		• Tech platforms allow for global collaboration, enabling voices from diverse communities to be heard.
11	Sustainable cities and communities	• Smart city technologies help optimise traffic management, reduce pollution and improve public services like waste management and water supply.
		• AI and data analytics enable urban planning that promotes green spaces and energy-efficient buildings.
		• IoT and sensors help in monitoring air quality and provide real-time information to citizens.
		• E-governance reduces reliance on paper-based administrative processes.

(Continued)

Table 6.2 (Continued)

#SDG	Description	Examples of computing's potential impact
12	Responsible consumption and production	• Circular economy models in tech promote recycling and sustainable production. • Blockchain technology helps track ethical sourcing of materials and ensure sustainability in supply chains. • AI and machine learning optimise production processes, minimising waste and energy consumption. • The right-to-repair movement extends product lifespan, reducing e-waste. • E-waste management solutions using IoT and data analytics ensure that electronic products are recycled responsibly.
13	Climate action	• Big data and AI enable better climate modelling, predict extreme weather events and guide policy decisions to combat climate change. • IoT devices in smart homes and cities monitor energy use and reduce carbon footprints. • Cloud computing and virtualisation reduce the energy consumption of data centres. • Digital platforms enable remote work, reducing travel-related carbon emissions.

(Continued)

Table 6.2 (Continued)

#SDG	Description	Examples of computing's potential impact
14	Life below water	• IoT sensors help monitor ocean health, track water quality and protect marine life. • Satellite data and AI assist in tracking overfishing, marine pollution and climate change impacts on ocean ecosystems. • Mobile apps and sensors raise awareness of marine conservation and promote sustainable fishing practices.
15	Life on land	• Drones and satellite imaging are used to monitor deforestation, track wildlife populations and enforce conservation efforts. • AI and machine learning can analyse data to predict biodiversity threats and help design conservation strategies. • IoT sensors monitor soil health and ecosystem dynamics, enabling sustainable land management.
16	Peace, justice and strong institutions	• Blockchain technology can improve transparency, prevent corruption and ensure accountability in governance. • Big data and AI help identify trends in human rights violations, enabling better legal frameworks and policy decisions.

(Continued)

Table 6.2 (Continued)

#SDG	Description	Examples of computing's potential impact
		• Digital platforms improve public access to legal resources, e-government services and citizen engagement.
17	Partnerships for the Goals	• Cloud computing facilitates global collaboration on sustainable development projects, enabling organisations to share data and resources effectively.
		• Big data and AI help track progress on the SDGs, ensuring that efforts are coordinated and evidence-based.
		• Digital platforms encourage global cooperation in research, innovation and the sharing of sustainable technologies.

MOVING TOWARD MORE ETHICAL AND SUSTAINABLE PRACTICES

To ensure technology benefits both people and the planet, multiple stakeholders must take action. Whilst most of these are significant steps, without trying to move forward on them there is no chance of improving things, let alone achieving them. So at whatever level, they are targets to aim for.

For companies

- Adopt sustainable product design with repairable and modular components as far as possible. This is potentially a large shift for many companies, where the financial model is often built around continuous expansion of features and regular upgrades and replacements (Lacy and Rutqvist, 2015).

- Consider how systems are designed and try to allow for the full technology lifecycle (TechDirect, 2024).

- Commit to carbon neutrality and transition to renewable energy sources: whilst many companies have these aspirations, doing this across all of their activity is another huge challenge when considering the different forms of carbon footprint.

- Improve supply chain transparency to ensure fair labour conditions and enable better tracking of things such as carbon emissions. There is some progress in this area, with more companies adopting transparency in their supply chains, and in looking to improve the conditions of those that work in the organisations that supply them.

- Ensure company sustainability policies encompass sustainable development in its fullest sense, and that IT is considered within that to reduce its negative impacts and maximise its benefits.

For governments and policymakers

- Enforce stricter e-waste recycling regulations, including both domestic and industrial waste. Improving routine access to recycling facilities for electronic goods and leading by example in minimising that need through better technology adoption and solutions.

- Provide incentives for green technology innovation to enable the transition to a sustainable society.

- Promote the right-to-repair laws to extend device lifespan for devices so that companies have to support their customers in prolonging the use of devices. This would need to encompass support for devices and operating systems, for example so that security patches are available.

For professionals

When considering solutions or developing them, think about the potential impact. Watch out for opportunities to support some of the SDGs, whether as part of the work or as voluntary activities. Some key steps for ethical and sustainable tech practices are:

- **Sustainable coding and development** – Write efficient code, use green hosting, minimise digital waste and support open-source sustainability projects.

- **Ethical AI and data use** – Reduce bias in AI, ensure transparency, protect user privacy and advocate for fair data practices.

- **Sustainable hardware and IT infrastructure** – Choose energy-efficient devices, extend hardware lifespan, support e-waste recycling and promote the circular economy.

- **Green IT and cloud computing** – Use carbon-neutral cloud providers, implement serverless architectures, monitor energy consumption and consider edge computing.

- **Workplace advocacy and ethical design** – Champion green IT policies, push for ethical tech policies, design for accessibility and avoid exploitative user interfaces.

- **Continuous learning and ethical development** – Stay informed, complete ethics and sustainability training, engage in ethical decision making and join ethical tech communities.

- Utilise suitable frameworks and approaches that can help to identify and address issues, such as the DIODE framework (described in Chapter 8).

- If you perceive damage or harm from your systems – particularly with respect to the environment or broader sustainability issues – raise them. This may be through internal processes, or if they seem inappropriate or dysfunctional, through external bodies as a whistleblower.

For individuals

Consumers play a crucial role in driving sustainable IT. Here are some practical steps individuals can take:

- **Extend the life of your devices** – Repair instead of replacing whenever possible.

- **Choose sustainable brands** – Support companies that prioritise ethical sourcing and energy efficiency.

- **Reduce digital waste** – Unsubscribe from unused cloud services and delete unnecessary data to lower the energy impact of data centres.

- **Recycle e-waste responsibly** – Donate old devices or use certified recycling programmes instead of throwing them away.

- **Use energy-efficient settings** – Lower screen brightness, enable power-saving modes and turn off unused devices.

Even small actions, when collectively adopted, can significantly reduce the environmental footprint of technology.

DISCUSSION

Sustainable computing is not just a technological challenge, it is a moral and ethical obligation. As digital technologies continue to shape our world, we must ensure they align with environmental and social responsibility. By integrating ethical practices, sustainable innovation and adherence to the UN SDGs, the tech industry can transform from a contributor to global challenges into a leader in sustainable progress. The responsibility lies with developers, businesses, policymakers and consumers to make choices that prioritise sustainability and long-term impact. Every action – from designing energy-efficient software to advocating for ethical production – helps create a future where technology serves both humanity and the planet. With some technology, the choice at times is not whether we can do something, but rather, should we? For example, where a technology has some benefit but may cause greater harm, we should consider that and raise concerns. Examples can include smart clothing or even blockchain for finance. These sorts of technologies do have many positive applications but are these greater than the negative impact? When it comes to online platforms and technologies we should consider the benefits and negative aspects before promoting them. Ultimately, the choices we make today will shape the digital world of tomorrow – let's ensure it is one that benefits all. We should look to maximise the use of computing to ensure that global good, recognising that for some aspects there may be differing views of what good is. For example, gender equality and access to health have political implications in our own work.

REFERENCES

Amnesty International. (2022) The Social Atrocity: Meta and the Right to Remedy for the Rohingya. London, UK: Amnesty International. Available from: amnesty.org/en/latest/news/2022/09/myanmar-facebooks-systems-promoted-violence-against-rohingya-meta-owes-reparations-new-report.

Balde, C.P., Forti, V., Gray, V., Kuehr, R. and Stegmann, P. (2017) The global e-waste monitor 2017: Quantities, flows and resources. Bonn, Germany/Geneva, Switzerland/Vienna, Austria: United Nations University, International Telecommunication Union & International Solid Waste Association.

Belkhir, L. and Elmeligi, A. (2018) 'Assessing ICT global emissions footprint: Trends to 2040 & recommendations'. *Journal of Cleaner Production*, 177. 448–463.

Floridi, L., Cowls, J., Beltrametti, M., Chatila, R., Chazerand, P., Dignum, V., Luetge, C., Madelin, R., Pagallo, U., Rossi, F. and Schafer, B. (2018) AI4People – an ethical framework for a good AI society: opportunities, risks, principles, and recommendations. *Minds and Machines*, 28. 689–707.

Forbes. (2023) One Year After The Merge: Sustainability Of Ethereum's Proof-Of-Stake Is Uncertain. Available from: forbes.com/sites/digital-assets/2023/10/11/one-year-after-the-merge-sustainability-of-ethereums-proof-of-stake-is-uncertain/.

Gogoll, J., Zuber, N., Kacianka, S., Greger, T., Pretschner, A. and Nida-Rümelin, J. (2021) Ethics in the software development process: from codes of conduct to ethical deliberation. *Philosophy & Technology*, 34. 1085–1108. Available at: link. springer.com/article/10.1007/s13347-021-00451-w.

Gordon, N. (2010) 'Sustainable information technology awareness'. *Innovation in Teaching and Learning in Information and Computer Sciences*, 9 (2). 1–4.

Gordon, N. (2014) Sustainable development as a framework for ethics and skills in higher education computing courses. In: *Integrative Approaches to Sustainable Development at University Level: Making the Links*. Cham, Switzerland: Springer International Publishing. 345–357.

iNews. (2025) At least 13 suicides may be linked to Horizon IT scandal. Available from: inews.co.uk/news/postmasters-may-have-killed-themselves-horizon-scandal-3793622.

ITU and World Bank (2023) Green data centers: towards a sustainable digital transformation. Available from: itu.int/en/ITU-D/Environment/Pages/Toolbox/Green-data-center-guide. aspx.

Lacy, P. and Rutqvist, J. (2015) *Waste to Wealth: The Circular Economy Advantage* (Vol. 91). London, UK: Palgrave Macmillan.

Larcker, D.F. and Tayan, B. (2024) Boeing 737 MAX: Organizational and Governance Failures. Stanford Graduate School of Business. Available from: corpgov.law.harvard. edu/2024/06/06/boeing-737-max.

Mobbs, P. (2012) A practical guide to sustainable IT. Association for Progressive Communications. Available from: apc.org/sites/default/files/PracticalGuideSustainableIT_Section_1.pdf.

Murugesan, S. and Gangadharan, G.R. (2012) *Harnessing Green IT: Principles and Practices*. Hoboken, NJ, USA: John Wiley & Sons. 1–21.

Oppenhoff. (2023) What Ever Happened to the Diesel Scandal? Current Developments and a Glimpse into the Future. Cologne, Germany: Oppenhoff & Partner. Available from: oppenhoff.eu/en/news/detail/what-ever-happened-to-the-diesel-scandal-current-developments-and-a-glimpse-into-the-future.

Podder, S. and Balani, N. (2024) Green software essentials: a Q&A guide for practitioners. Green Software Foundation. Available from: greensoftware.foundation/articles/reading-list-on-green-software.

Proske, M., Sánchez, D., Clemm, C. and Baur, S. (2020) Life cycle assessment of the Fairphone 3. Berlin, Germany: Fraunhofer Institute for Reliability and Microintegration (IZM). Available from: fairphone.com/wp-content/uploads/2020/07/Fairphone_3_LCA.pdf.

Sachs, J.D. (2015) *The Age of Sustainable Development*. New York, NY, USA: Columbia University Press.

Selwyn, N. (2004) Reconsidering political and popular understandings of the digital divide. *New Media & Society*, 6 (3). 341–362.

Software AG. (2023) A guide to sustainable IT. Available at: softwareag.com/content/dam/softwareag/global/resource-library/alfabet/guide/sustainable-it/guide-sustainable-it-en.pdf.

Software Improvement Group. (2024) The complete guide to green computing. Available from: softwareimprovementgroup.com/publications/complete-guide-to-green-computing.

TechDirect. (2024) Adopting sustainable IT practices: a comprehensive guide. Available from: techdirect.net/blog/adopting-sustainable-it-practices-a-comprehensive-guide.

The Guardian. (2025) Google's emissions up 51% as AI electricity demand derails efforts to go green. Available from: theguardian.com/technology/2025/jun/27/google-emissions-ai-electricity-demand-derail-efforts-green.

UN (United Nations). (2022) The Sustainable Development Goals Report 2022. Available from: unstats.un.org/sdgs/report/2022/.

Vanli, T. (2024) Ranking of global smart cities using dynamic factor analysis. *Social Indicators Research*, 171 (2). 405–437.

Williams, W. (2025) Post Office Horizon IT Inquiry: Volume 1 – Human Impact and Redress. London, UK: UK Government. Available from: postofficehorizoninquiry.org.uk.

Wired. (2016) Google's DeepMind trains AI to cut its energy bills by 40%. Available from: wired.com/story/google-deepmind-data-centres-efficiency/.

7 NAVIGATING EMERGING TECHNOLOGIES

Catherine Flick

Given the earlier exploration of ethics and current technologies and issues, in this chapter we explore the opportunities and challenges of new technologies. First we outline the ethical turbulence surrounding emerging technologies, highlighting the persistent influence of corporate interests, regulatory gaps and conceptual confusion. We then explore related ethical concerns – including hype, privacy, security, autonomy, societal impact, responsibility and uncertainty of outcomes – into practical guidance for technology practitioners. The third part acknowledges the limits of individual agency within large organisations and provides strategies for ethical influence, collective action and professional accountability, with guidance on how to embrace ethical responsibility.

We live in a time of rapidly changing technological landscapes. Billionaires run tech companies according to their whims, regardless of the impact on anything other than share prices or personal wealth. Governments enable technology companies to take advantage of their citizens by sharing data without adequate security or privacy controls, or fail to regulate ethically problematic technologies, choosing instead to let the companies involved sweep the societal effects of their products under the carpet. Untested and unproven technologies put people in danger, and it seems like there is nowhere left to go for tech companies or tech professionals who want to behave ethically – it's join them or die. With hype cycles and disruptive technologies dominating the discussions around technology, and limited regulation, education or protection of society from its effects, the fabric of society is dramatically changing in a technocentric manner. With such a dramatic shift in priorities, what is an ethical professional to do?

This may seem a grim picture to paint. But it is also reflective of how technology has always developed – historical cases presented in Chapter 4, for example, show the impacts of unethical developments and, ultimately, the costs to their developers as well as individuals and society. Back in 1985, James Moor's *What is Computer Ethics?* outlined the policy 'vacuums' and conceptual 'muddles' that arise in the development of new technologies, and that computer ethics is the way to help navigate these. Additionally, he identified that one of the most problematic issues around computers is the 'invisibility factor' – which can generate conceptual vacuums as well as cause issues of trust in the outputs we see (Moor, 1985). This invisibility factor and its impacts, too, have not fundamentally changed. We use a lot of technology that we do not understand the workings of, and we assume that the outputs we are being given are accurate, when, as we have seen in previous chapters, they are not.

With technology continually advancing, one might expect that the ethical issues continue to advance. However, the opposite is true – the ethical issues are surprisingly stable; it is their application that tends to shift with each technology. For example, privacy is a long-standing ethical expectation that is still a frequent occurrence with modern computing technologies. The Convention 108(+) for the protection of individuals with regard to the processing of personal data recently celebrated its 40th anniversary (Council of Europe, 2021). What 'privacy' looked like back in 1981 is very different from how it looks today, with massive, often centralised data lakes that are increasingly interconnected and used for purposes that are not always transparent or accessible (Lovato et al., 2023). The expectation of security is another. In the 1980s, security was largely about physical security; these days it is more associated with surveillance technologies, data protection and secure infrastructures, and is an expected fundamental building block of any new technology.

New ethical issues have emerged over time, however. For example, it was identified when rewriting the Association of Computing Machinery's *Code of Ethics* (originally published in 1992, updated in 2018) that some new ethical issues had arisen as a result of the interconnectedness of technologies and their increasing melding into the fabric of society (Brinkman et al., 2016). Similarly, the impact of the retirement of systems, such as in the case of Microsoft's retirement of earlier versions of Windows that caused significant consternation, was added into the 2018 version of the Code (Gotterbarn et al., 2017). This change reflected the change in the technology industry itself – from a set of software companies that sold specific software products that were maintained as long as necessary, to companies that were chasing ever-increasing amounts of growth of both customer bases and income. It may be that in future, as technologies, business strategies, and user and consumer behaviours change, that new ethical issues will emerge.

It is in this spirit that this chapter will look at some of the key ethical issues common to emerging technologies and put forward useful guidance for these.

A comprehensive and evidence-based set of ethical issues for emerging technologies exists (Stahl et al., 2017), although it targets its assessment at policymakers and researchers, not practitioners. Despite this, many of the issues identified are appropriate for practitioners to consider as well, and this chapter will reframe the identified ethical issues in this context. It is important for the reader to understand that each of these issues has an extremely complex and deeply discussed history within computing technologies. The following discussion is but a very high-level summary of that discussion, framed specifically to help practitioners think through the ethical issues that are most likely to be encountered when working with or creating emerging technologies.

The key ethical issues that will be addressed in the next section are conceptual issues and hype, privacy, security, autonomy, treatment of humans and society, responsibility, and uncertainty of outcomes. This is not an exhaustive list of discussion points but a starting point, and it is likely that trade-offs will need to be made. The last section of this chapter will provide further information on where you can find more frameworks, activities and assessment criteria for helping to identify ethical issues in emerging technologies.

CONCEPTUAL ISSUES AND HYPE

If we think about how 'artificial intelligence' is being used today, it is a prime example of Moor's 'conceptual muddle'. 'AI' could mean anything from a simple algorithm that determines the shortest route to a destination in your sat-nav, or the way a monster in a video game behaves, or a complex chatbot that responds to your innermost desires, to an app that makes deepfake videos of political figures. Similar conceptual issues arise around other emerging technologies due to their complexities – such as 'crypto' (as in blockchain-based cryptocurrencies) and 'quantum' (as in anything to do with quantum computing). These form a kind of 'invisibility factor' of their own by masking the complexity and muddling the concepts between what might be useful or socially acceptable and what might be harmful or socially unacceptable. Similarly, it is often complex to understand how these new technologies are funded – whether by venture capital, experimental arms of large companies or government-grant-funded university spin-offs, for example. All of these conceptual issues help spur the hype cycle, as the complexity can be hidden behind potential future possibilities rather than what is possible with the technology now.

If you are working in emerging technologies:

- Find a way to explain how your technology works to people without expertise, especially for those who might be impacted by your technology.

- Be open and transparent about how it is funded and the plans for future, sustainable monetisation.

- Actively help to deconstruct hype that might surround the emerging technology (especially that which relies on potential future possibilities that are not currently possible), even if it is financially beneficial for you to be part of the hype.

- Have a plan for what happens when your technology is no longer in the growth stages – what are the long-term sustainability and end of life plans?

PRIVACY

As discussed earlier, privacy is a long-held ethical issue in the realm of technology. Those working with emerging technologies need to be aware of privacy requirements not just in law, but within the communities their technologies are affecting. Higher degrees of complexity of the technology and sensitivity of the personal information being used require increased responsibility towards those whose information is being collected. There may be people who are impacted by your technologies that actively do not want to use them, are not interested in them or assist others in using them. These people also need to be protected, not just those deemed 'users'.

If you are working in emerging technologies, you should do the following:

- Conduct full privacy evaluations of what is required for trust in your technology by the communities your technology might impact, not just 'users'.

- Don't just meet the requirements of the law, but exceed them.

- Be especially mindful towards those who might be particularly vulnerable.

- Push back against 'scope creep' which might push against the boundaries established in your privacy evaluation.

SECURITY

New technologies bring with them new vectors for security vulnerabilities, whether through the technology itself or through an interface with humans. We have seen the changes that generative AI has brought to identity theft and phishing attacks, for example, and quantum computing has the potential to break current security methods entirely. Understanding how current security practices are applicable to the emerging technology is extremely important, as is whether or not the technology itself is likely to change current practice. Security can also mean physical security – infrastructure is increasingly a target of attack these days, and large infrastructure projects in unstable parts of the world (whether physically or societally), if impacted, could cause significant knock-on effects. Even climate change can have an extreme effect here – security of energy infrastructure needs to be an ongoing concern for any company that has technology embedded in the fabric of society.

If you are working in emerging technologies:

- Consider the locations of any infrastructure and their long-term suitability and sustainability.

- Remain vigilant to unexpected security-related uses and abuses of the technology and be ready to mitigate or change the technology to address them.

- If the technology is likely to break existing security measures, ensure there is a plan in place for migration away that does not open up a gap that is directly exploitable by bad actors.

AUTONOMY

Technologies can often take control away from humans through methods such as surveillance, behaviour modification, decision making, mood shifting, and so on. These can be both positive (for example, public health) and negative (for example, automated decision making). This may also be accompanied by requirements by the government, workplaces, schools or other service providers to use the technology to access services or conduct work.

If you are working in emerging technologies:

- Be open and transparent about how your technology takes away from or provides autonomy to the people it impacts; don't just focus on the benefits.

- Have easy, graded and transparent ways of opting in or out of autonomy-changing aspects of your technology that aren't just 'don't use it' options; this may be impossible in practice.

- If your technology makes decisions instead of humans, have a plan for dealing with unfair decisions, decisions that are made as a result of bias or decisions that might otherwise harm or cause problems for a human.

- Accept that you may have to change aspects of your technology to ensure that people's autonomy is protected.

HUMANS AND SOCIETY

Here we see again our 'invisibility factor' – most humans will not understand what is happening behind the curtain of technology or understand fully the impact it might have on them or on society. Often, technology developers do not have a full grasp of what the impacts might be either. This does not absolve them from the responsibility for managing these impacts, however – this is an ongoing process throughout the development and deployment of emerging technologies. Some people may not be able to have access to or use of your technology, even if it is mandated by workplaces or government. Accessibility is extremely important not just for long-term sustainability of technologies, but for marginalised groups that may not usually be supported. This includes not just users with varying degrees of disability but also those with varying degrees of access to technology. Many emerging technologies also impact the role of humans within society: disruptive technologies are especially impactful here. If your technology is likely to have a significant impact on the role of humans within society – through employment, education, human relationships or even fundamental philosophical questions around what it is to be human – it needs to ensure that overall, mitigating the potential for harm to human and societal impacts takes priority over any other consideration.

If you are working in emerging technologies:

- Have a plan for how to handle new potential harmful uses or applications of your technology, and be vigilant about watching for these.

- Be proactive about incorporating marginalised groups, such as those with disabilities, limited access to technology or other inequalities, into the development process and regularly check in to ensure their expectations are being met.

- Ensure that any technology that replaces humans in terms of labour, relationships or other aspects of human life has robust mechanisms for humans to challenge and help to positively change the development or deployment of the technology.

- Don't take advantage of political vacuums that may allow legal grey areas for harmful applications of the technology to exist, even if they are of financial benefit.

- Don't anthropomorphise technology; be clear about its origins, limitations, and benefits and disadvantages in neutral terminology in order to be as open and transparent with humans as possible.

RESPONSIBILITY

Systems are so complex these days that it is hard to know who might be responsible for any consequences of the system. This is often called the 'problem of many hands' (van de Poel et al., 2015). With technologies increasingly making decisions in place of humans, this exacerbates the difficulty in allocation of responsibility. Sometimes this can be limited to the legal notion of legal liability, but this is not always useful either. Extremely large companies that have many other subsidiaries underneath them also make this more difficult. And it speaks to you, the reader, too, as to where you should be placing your efforts best in order to ensure ethical creation and deployment of technology. Some technologies might help in the ascription of responsibility, such as tracking software or other surveillance technologies, but these may come at a cost of autonomy or privacy.

If you are working in emerging technologies:

- 'Many hands' might make light work, but ensure that there is a chain of responsibility for each decision that is made during the development process and deployment.

- If the technology has automated decision-making processes, ensure these are well documented, transparent and explainable to the human about which a decision has been made.

- Take responsibility for the work and the outcomes of the work that you do.

UNCERTAINTY OF OUTCOMES

The nature of emerging technologies is such that we do not always know what the impacts might be. There is usually a dominant narrative around the positive and beneficial outcomes of the technology, but less around what the negative outcomes and disadvantages might be. This is often a deliberate effort on the part of the developers to secure funding, draw in an initial userbase and develop some hype around the technology. However, this can also cause developers to create a 'bubble' around themselves that allows them to avoid thinking critically about the technology. Some of these bubbles can also build up fictional possible futures where the technology might go, without evidence that there is the capability for it to do so. In the current hype cycles around generative AI we have seen this in the discussions around artificial general intelligence, artificial superintelligence and similar, none of which is currently possible given existing technology. This hyping of future possibilities also drove a lot of the crypto-asset rush, leading to significant negative consequences as the bubble burst (Flick, 2022). It is therefore imperative that developers of technology do not overhype their product and remain able to take on critical assessments of the potentials for harm. Keeping informed on expert critical opinions is likely to help identify new applications of existing ethical issues to the technology or in identifying new ethical issues as well.

If you are working in emerging technologies:

- Engage in activities that attempt to elicit future possible harmful applications or uses of the technology, and mitigations or design decisions that help to avoid them.

- Engage with different potential populations of affected users (and non-users) to develop understandings of their expectations around the technology.

- Hire a diverse set of developers and give them space and power to be critical within the development lifecycle.

- Keep abreast of expert critical voices about the technology and mitigate or avoid the issues they are critical of.

HOW TO USE THESE SUGGESTIONS

For those who are in positions of decision-making power, great! You should help to shape the technology your company develops and deploys in the ways outlined above. However, it is important to recognise that, as an individual, if you are employed by a large corporation, you are often not in a position to make the kinds of decisions that the above advice is useful for. There are several ways that you can help to influence decision making within your company; some of these may be risky in terms of job security, however.

If you are working in emerging technologies but without decision-making powers:

- Keep up to date on the discussions around the emerging technology you are working on, particularly the critical discussions, and try to influence incorporation of those criticisms into the development process.

- Join a professional organisation and join in with their efforts to develop policy and lobby for regulation around emerging technologies.

- Join a union and get involved to keep companies accountable to their workers.

- Push back against requests to do unethical work – you can use your professional organisation's code of ethics as a benchmark for professionalism.

- Attempt to drive in-house change by organising a movement to push back against unethical technology (such as Googlers did against Project Dragonfly (Gallagher, 2018)) or promote ethical technology development.

- Use whistleblowing protections and procedures to call attention to significant ethical breaches.

- Report members of professional organisations to their organisation if they are in violation of that organisation's code of ethics.

- Continue to take responsibility for your own work and the outcomes of that work; hold yourself to higher standards if necessary.

It is important for society to have a strong voice in what emerging technologies are developed and how they are deployed and used. We are increasingly seeing a significant imbalance between society and technology companies – instead of developing technology that responds to societal needs, they are developing technologies with (often) little actual utility, which can be hyped up to produce value to shareholders. Ethical technology companies can do their part by resisting as many of these perfidious mechanisms as possible; this chapter has attempted to assist with that discussion by suggesting ways to ensure emerging technologies are developed with an ethical eye.

REFERENCES

Brinkman, B., Gotterbarn, D., Miller, K. and Wolf, M.J. (2016) 'Making a positive impact: updating the ACM code of ethics'. *Communications of the ACM*, 59 (12). 7–13. Available from: doi. org/10.1145/3015149.

Council of Europe. (2021) Convention 108 and Protocols – Data Protection, Data Protection. Available from: coe.int/en/web/data-protection/convention108-and-protocol.

Flick, C. (2022) 'A critical professional ethical analysis of non-fungible tokens (NFTs)'. *Journal of Responsible Technology*. 100054. Available from: doi.org/10.1016/j.jrt.2022.100054.

Gallagher, R. (2018) 'Google Staff Tell Bosses China Censorship Is "Moral and Ethical" Crisis'. *The Intercept*. Available from: theintercept.com/2018/08/16/google-china-crisis-staff-dragonfly/.

Gotterbarn, D., Bruckman, A., Flick, C., Miller, K. and Wolf, M.J. (2017) 'ACM code of ethics: a guide for positive action'. *Communications of the ACM*, 61 (1). 121–128. Available from: doi.org/10.1145/3173016.

Lovato, J., Mueller, P., Suchdev, P. and Dodds, P.S. (2023) More Data Types More Problems: A Temporal Analysis of Complexity, Stability, and Sensitivity in Privacy Policies. In: *2023 ACM Conference on Fairness Accountability and Transparency. FAccT '23: the 2023 ACM Conference on Fairness, Accountability, and Transparency*. Chicago, IL, USA: ACM. 1088–1100. Available from: doi.org/10.1145/3593013.3594065.

Moor, J.H. (1985) 'What is computer ethics?' *Metaphilosophy*, 16 (4). 266–275.

van de Poel, I., Royakkers, L. and Zwart, S.D. (2015) *Moral Responsibility and the Problem of Many Hands*. London, UK; New York, NY, USA: Routledge, Taylor & Francis Group (Routledge studies in ethics and moral theory, 29).

Stahl, B., Timmermans, J. and Flick, C. (2017) 'Ethics of emerging information and communication technologies on the implementation of responsible research and innovation'. *Science and Public Policy*, 44 (3). 369–381. Available from: doi. org/10.1093/scipol/scw069.

8 FUTURE DIRECTIONS IN TECH ETHICS

Neil Gordon

In this closing chapter we outline potential next steps. Recognising the accelerating pace of technological change and the urgent need for ethics to evolve from reactive postmortems to proactive design, it explores the shift from individual ethical champions to a culture of shared responsibility, where ethical fluency becomes a core professional skill across roles and sectors. The third part introduces adaptive methodologies – like scenario planning and participatory foresight – that help navigate emerging technologies and unpredictable futures. The fourth revisits foundational ethical questions in light of new frontiers such as AI-generated art and ambient surveillance. The fifth offers practical guidance for readers to continue their ethical development, highlighting tools like the DIODE framework, CPD opportunities and community engagement – reminding us that ethical tech is not just about what we build, but who we become in the process.

We live in rapidly changing times for technology. Every few months we see a new tool, a new platform or a new ethical dilemma arising from the intersection of human ambition and technological power. We were used to tech developing rapidly but incrementally, whilst now it is evolving by disruption. So where does that leave tech ethics?

It leaves it busier than ever. But also, more hopeful – if we're ready to engage in a pro-active way. For tech ethics, this means anticipatory ethics, not just reactive. Too often, ethics has been treated as a post-mortem. A reflection after failure or a line in a policy doc no one reads. But the direction of travel is changing. More organisations are embracing anticipatory ethics, where ethical thinking is woven in before the system is even built.

This means incorporating horizon-scanning into project design: asking who might be harmed, whose voices are missing and what unintended consequences may emerge. Tools like Responsible Research and Innovation (RRI), ethical impact assessments or stakeholder co-creation are becoming part of the practical toolkit.

From the few to the many

Right now, ethical leadership in tech often rests with champions – one or two voices in a room reminding others of the human consequences. But in the future, this needs to be normalised with ethical awareness across roles, sectors and seniority levels. That means everyone from interns to executives sees ethics not as someone else's job, but as part of their role and responsibility.

Training in ethics should not be a bolt-on but a key part of professional development, hiring expectations and organisational reward structures. Just as we value technical competence, we'll value ethical fluency.

Adapting to the unexpected

Emerging technologies – from synthetic media to quantum computing – will surface problems we can't fully anticipate. So, the future of tech ethics lies in methodologies that flex: scenario planning, value-sensitive design, participatory foresight. These help us act responsibly even when the terrain is unfamiliar. The goal isn't to have a rulebook for every new technology; it's to build the habits of reflection, inclusion and accountability that guide good choices, even in uncharted territory.

New frontiers, old questions

AI-generated art, brain-computer interfaces, ambient biometric surveillance – none of these are science fiction anymore. As we push further into such domains, old questions take on new urgency. What counts as harm? Who gets to decide? Where does consent live in ambient environments?

We need to revisit our existing ethical frameworks, codes of conduct and laws with critical eyes and plural perspectives. Ethics won't be a static checklist but an evolving conversation, shaped by global voices and real-world impacts.

FUTURE DIRECTIONS FOR YOU: CONTINUING YOUR ETHICAL DEVELOPMENT

This book has offered questions, tools and insights to support ethical practice. But its final message is simple: ethical tech isn't just about the systems we build – it's about the people we become while building them.

Ethical awareness isn't a one-off achievement, it's a professional habit. As technology evolves, so too must our understanding of its implications. Whether you're just starting out in tech, or are looking to deepen your established practice, here are some practical ways to continue your journey in tech ethics.

Frameworks and guidelines

Firstly, explore and utilise some of the existing frameworks and guidelines that can aid in identifying and addressing ethical issues. In addition to the suggestions in the preceding chapters, try the DIODE Framework.

The Diode Framework

The **DIODE framework**, which emerged from work by the BCS Ethics Strategic Panel, is a structured, five-stage approach to assessing the ethical dimensions of new technologies. It guides you through the following steps:

1. **Define questions** – Frame the ethical issues with a clear definition of the technology or project being examined.

2. **Issues analysis** – Consider all the different stake-holder perspectives and risks.

3. **Options evaluation** – Explore possible actions and safeguards to ensure relevant choices are made.

4. **Decision determination** – Make and justify your ethical choice, including what may lead to it being reconsidered with future changes.

5. **Explanations dissemination** – Communicate your reasoning transparently and to the right people, which may include the public domain.

DIODE is a practical tool for individuals and teams, especially when navigating complex or emerging tech.

Source: Harris, I., Jennings, R., Pullinger, D., Rogerson, S., and Duquenoy, P. (2011) 'Ethical assessment of new technologies: a meta-methodology'. *Journal of Information*, 9 (1). 49–64.

Explore CPD

There are numerous continuing professional development options. For example, BCS offers a range of courses (some free, some paid) that can help you build ethical fluency. Some of the more relevant ones to this book are:

- **The Ethical IT Professional** (Free for BCS members) – A short, accessible course introducing the ethical responsibilities of IT practitioners. A good starting point to consider the BCS Code of Conduct and understanding your role in upholding professional standards.

- **BCS Foundation Certificate in the Ethical Build of AI** (Paid-for course) – A 12-hour on-demand course that explores how to design and deploy AI systems responsibly. It covers data ethics, regulatory frameworks and practical safeguards. Ideal for developers, data scientists and project leads.

These sort of courses can contribute to your CPD and can be used to demonstrate your commitment to ethical practice, whether for chartership, promotion or personal growth.

Make ethics part of your practice

Other ways you can explore these topics and support your own development include:

- **Join a professional group** – For example, BCS and non-BCS members engage with BCS specialist groups or local chapters focused on ethics, AI or green computing.

- **Reflect regularly** – Use tools like DIODE or ethical checklists in project retrospectives.

- **Mentor or be mentored** – Share your learning or seek guidance from others navigating similar challenges.

- **Stay informed** – Follow developments in tech ethics through journals, podcasts and conferences.

Ethics isn't just about what you know – it's about what you **do**. So, keep learning, keep questioning and keep building a tech future that's not just innovative, but also just. Stay curious. Stay critical. Stay kind. Ethics doesn't end with this book – it begins with what you do after reading it.

GLOSSARY

This book is aimed at IT practitioners and managers, and so IT terms such as 'integration testing' or 'project lifecycle' are not included in the Glossary as they are assumed to be familiar to the readers.

AI: Artificial intelligence; a range of IT technologies including machine learning and neural networks which have the common property of making decisions or recommendations based on some form of statistical algorithm (as opposed to rules), at least in part.

ACM: Association for Computing Machinery is a US-based international learned society for computing – see acm.org/

Autonomy: The right or freedom of self government (countries) or of action (human beings) or of action (robots and AI systems).

BCS, The Chartered Institute for IT: formerly the British Computer Society, professional body for IT practitioners – see bcs.org/

Blockchain: A form of a more generalised technology called distributed ledger (DLT). DLT is a database where no single person or organisation controls the data, but rather there are multiple copies of the data owned and run by different parties and a new record is created on the database when all the owners agree that the change has been made. Blockchain is one of the mechanisms by which the databases build consensus on a change. For more on DLT see: en.wikipedia. org/wiki/Distributed_ledger; on Blockchain see en.wikipedia. org/wiki/Blockchain

Bernard Madoff: An American investment fund manager who defrauded investors of billions of dollars in the funds he ran. For more information see: investopedia.com/terms/b/bernard-madoff.asp.

Boeing 737 scandal: A scandal based on two Boeing 737 Max crashes which killed many people and was ultimately based on a faulty flight control system. For more information see: en.wikipedia.org/wiki/Boeing_737_MAX_groundings

Cambridge Analytica: A software company that unethically harvested Facebook data to target political advertising. For more information see: researchgate.net/publication/330032180_Cambridge_Analytica_Ethics_And_Online_Manipulation_With_Decision-Making_Process

CEN: The European Committee for Standardization is an association that brings together the national standardisation bodies of 34 European countries. For more information see: cencenelec.eu/about-cen/

Citizens' Jury: A gathering of up to two-dozen diverse individuals, who come together to engage in open, respectful dialogue on complex and meaningful topics. These groups are especially valuable when addressing issues that involve conflicting values, uncertain evidence, or significant ethical and societal consequences. The aim is to foster mutual understanding and shared perspectives to find a common position. For more information see: involve.org.uk/resource/citizens-jury

Convention 108+: A European Council convention created in 1981, Convention 108+ contains important innovations: it proclaims the importance of protecting the right to informational autonomy and human dignity in the face of technological developments. For more information see: coe.int/en/web/data-protection/convention108-and-protocol

Cryptocurrency: A type of digital token that has value and is based on a DLT database. As a result of being based on DLT, the currency is not dependent on nor subject to control by any single authority. This is in contrast to currencies issued by central banks or governments. Bitcoin is the leading example of a cryptocurrency. For more information on cryptocurrency see: en.wikipedia.org/wiki/Cryptocurrency and on Bitcoin see: en.wikipedia.org/wiki/Bitcoin

Deontological Ethics: A group of ethical theories that emphasise the idea that certain actions are good or bad, independent of the ends pursued and independent of the character of the actor. See Chapter 2.

Design Charrettes: A focused, collaborative workshop where a group of people from varied fields and the community come together to co-create design ideas. Unlike conventional consultation methods, this approach centres on design itself, encouraging hands-on exploration and shared creativity. For more information see: involve.org.uk/resource/design-charrettes

Dilemma: A situation in which a difficult choice has to be made between two or more alternatives, especially ones that are equally undesirable.

Dragonfly: A project in Google to develop a search engine compatible with China's state censorship rules, which caused an employee revolt. For more information see: en.wikipedia. org/wiki/Dragonfly_(search_engine)

e-learning and EdTech: The terms e-learning and EdTech are often used interchangeably. They represent distinct concepts within the broader field of education. E-learning refers to the delivery of educational content through electronic means, such as online courses or digital materials, while EdTech (Educational Technology) encompasses the industry and tools used to facilitate and enhance the learning experience through technology.

e-health and Healthtech: e-health is a subset of Healthtech focusing on the application of information and communication technologies (ICT) to support health and healthcare services, while Healthtech broadly encompasses all technologies used to improve healthcare.

Enron: A large US energy company that went bankrupt because of practices at the company of falsifying accounts. For more information see: en.wikipedia.org/wiki/Enron_scandal

Ethics: A branch of philosophy, often called moral philosophy, concerned with right and wrong, good and bad. More in Chapter 2.

Ethics Sandbox: Particularly in the context of AI, this is a controlled environment where AI systems can be developed, tested and validated before being released to the public. For more information see for example: dl.acm.org/doi/10.1145/3686038.3686049 or papers.ssrn.com/sol3/papers.cfm?abstract_id=4609613

Fujitsu: A large Japanese IT software, hardware and services group.

GDPR: General Data Protection Regulations; a set of EU data privacy regulations that was adopted by the UK and which in the UK was supplemented by the Data Protection Act 2018.

Horizon: A software program to support Post Office accounting in the UK, written by Fujitsu.

IEEE: Institute of Electrical and Electronics Engineers; the global community for technology professionals. For more information see: ieee.org/

IOT: Internet of Things; the idea that devices connect to the internet and communicate across it without human intervention (e.g. to provide status information or maintenance needs). For more information see: en.wikipedia.org/wiki/Internet_of_things

Moral Pluralism: The idea that there can be conflicting moral views that are each worthy of respect. For more information see: ethicsunwrapped.utexas.edu/glossary or plato.stanford.edu/entries/value-pluralism/

Post Office: The organisation that runs the network of post offices in the UK (different from the organisation that delivers letters and parcels, called the Royal Mail).

Professional: In this book, it is used in two senses: as a noun, a person who is a qualified member of a professional body; as an adjective, the behaviour expected of a member of a profession.

Quantum Computing: An emerging computing technology that uses quantum physics properties of entanglement and superposition to perform calculations. The idea is that, if successful, these computers will be orders of magnitude faster at certain types of calculation than current computers based on binary arithmetic. For more information see: en.wikipedia. org/wiki/Quantum_computing

Responsible Research and Innovation (RRI): A term used by the European Union's Framework Programmes to describe scientific research and technological development processes that take into account effects and potential impacts on the environment and society. For more information see: en.wikipedia.org/wiki/Responsible_Research_and_Innovation

Rights: The ability for a person to be free to do certain things (e.g. the right to go about one's daily business without being spied on). It places an obligation on the rest of society not to infringe on that person's freedom to do that thing.

Rohingya: This refers to the religious and ethnic minority in Myanmar that has been persecuted in that country by the government and army. The claim is that Facebook and its algorithms stoked the anti-Rohingya feelings in that country. For more information see: amnesty.org/en/latest/news/2022/09/myanmar-facebooks-systems-promoted-violence-against-rohingya-meta-owes-reparations-new-report/

Synthetic Media: Any media content, including images, videos, audio, and text, that is generated or manipulated using AI and machine learning techniques. For more information see: en.wikipedia.org/wiki/Synthetic_media

Telemedical or Telemedicine: Refers to the delivery of healthcare services and information using electronic communication and information technologies, enabling remote patient and clinician contact, care, advice, education and monitoring.

Teleological Ethics: A name for the group of ethical theories that emphasises the ends (or consequences) of actions as what defines good. More in Chapter 2.

UNSDG, sometimes shortened to SDG: United Nations Sustainable Development Goals. More in Chapter 6 and the list here: undp.org/sustainable-development-goals

UNDHR: United Nations' Universal Declaration of Human Rights. More in Chapter 6. For the full list see: un.org/en/about-us/universal-declaration-of-human-rights.

Virtue Ethics: An ethical theory that emphasises the development of good character and good personal traits. See Chapter 2.

VW: Volkswagen Audi Group. A large German-based motor vehicle manufacturer that was involved in a scandal whereby car software was programmed to trick emissions tests. For more information see: en.wikipedia.org/wiki/Volkswagen_emissions_scandal

LIST OF TABLES

LIST OF CASE STUDIES

PROFESSIONAL BODIES AND CODES OF CONDUCT/PRACTICE

- BCS, The Chartered Institute for IT (BCS): bcs.org/
- BCS Code of Conduct for members – ethics for IT professionals: bcs.org/membership-and-registrations/become-a-member/bcs-code-of-conduct/
- International Federation of Information Processing (IFIP): ifip.org/
- IFIP Code of Ethics: ifip.org/Reports/IFIP-Code-of-Ethics.pdf
- Institute of Electrical and Electronics Engineers (IEEE) – The world's largest technical professional organisation dedicated to advancing technology for the benefit of humanity: ieee.org/
- IEEE Code of Conduct: ieee.org/about/corporate/governance/code-of-conduct
- IEEE Code of Ethics: ieee.org/content/dam/ieee-org/ieee/web/org/about/corporate/ieee-code-of-ethics.pdf
- Association of Computing Machinery (ACM): acm.org/
- ACM Code of Ethics: acm.org/code-of-ethics
- The Joint ACM/IEEE-CS Software Engineering code of ethics and professional practice: acm.org/code-of-ethics/software-engineering-code/
- Institute of Engineering and Technology (IET): theiet.org/
- IET Rules of Conduct: theiet.org/about/governance/rules-of-conduct

The right of Gillian Arnold, Darren Dalcher, Catherine Flick, Neil Gordon, Bernd Carsten Stahl and Robert Tripp to be identified as authors of this work has been asserted by them in accordance with sections 77 and 78 of the Copyright, Designs and Patents Act 1988.

Published by BCS Learning and Development Ltd, a wholly owned subsidiary of BCS, The Chartered Institute for IT, 3 Newbridge Square, Swindon, SN1 1BY, UK.
bcs.org

EU GPSR Authorised Representative: LOGOS EUROPE, 9 Rue Nicolas Poussin, 17000 La Rochelle, France.
Contact@logoseurope.eu

Paperback ISBN: 978-1-78017-6802
PDF ISBN: 978-1-78017-6819
ePUB ISBN: 978-1-78017-6826

Ebook available

British Cataloguing in Publication Data.
A CIP catalogue record for this book is available at the British Library.

Disclaimer:

Publisher's acknowledgements
Reviewers: Nell Watson and Neil Taylor
Publisher: Ian Borthwick
Commissioning editor: Heather Wood
Production manager: Florence Leroy
Project manager: Just Content
Copy-editor: Just Content
Proofreader: Just Content
Cover design: Alex Wright
Cover image: iStock – StationaryTraveller
Sales director: Charles Rumball
Typeset by Lapiz Digital Services, Chennai, India

BCS, THE CHARTERED INSTITUTE FOR IT

BCS, The Chartered Institute for IT, is committed to making IT good for society. We use the power of our network to bring about positive, tangible change. We champion the global IT profession and the interests of individuals, engaged in that profession, for the benefit of all.

Exchanging IT expertise and knowledge
The Institute fosters links between experts from industry, academia and business to promote new thinking, education and knowledge sharing.

Supporting practitioners
Through continuing professional development and a series of respected IT qualifications, the Institute seeks to promote professional practice tuned to the demands of business. It provides practical support and information services to its members and volunteer communities around the world.

Setting standards and frameworks
The Institute collaborates with government, industry and relevant bodies to establish good working practices, codes of conduct, skills frameworks and common standards. It also offers a range of consultancy services to employers to help them adopt best practice.

Become a member
Over 70,000 people including students, teachers, professionals and practitioners enjoy the benefits of BCS membership. These include access to an international community, invitations to a roster of local and national events, career development tools and a quarterly thought-leadership magazine. Visit bcs.org to find out more.

Further information
BCS, The Chartered Institute for IT,
3 Newbridge Square,
Swindon, SN1 1BY, United Kingdom.
T +44 (0) 1793 417 417
(Monday to Friday, 09:00 to 17:00 UK time)
bcs.org/contact

shop.bcs.org/
publishing@bcs.uk

bcs.org/qualifications-and-certifications/
certifications-for-professionals/

Elevate your AI impact with the

BCS Foundation Certificate in the Ethical Build of AI

Your practical pathway to mastering AI ethics, from principles to real-world decisions.

- Developed with industry experts
- Globally recognised certification
- 5 x 90 minute self-paced modules
- Online training and exam
- £170 + VAT